THE BIOTECHNOLOGY REVOLUTION

GENETIC TESTING AND GENE THERAPY

EDITED BY JAMES WOLFE

Published in 2016 by Britannica Educational Publishing (a trademark of Encyclopædia Britannica, Inc.) in association with The Rosen Publishing Group, Inc.

29 East 21st Street, New York, NY 10010

Copyright © 2016 by Encyclopædia Britannica, Inc. Britannica, Encyclopædia Britannica, and the Thistle logo are registered trademarks of Encyclopædia Britannica, Inc. All rights reserved.

Rosen Publishing materials copyright © 2016 The Rosen Publishing Group, Inc. All rights reserved.

Distributed exclusively by Rosen Publishing.

To see additional Britannica Educational Publishing titles, go to rosenpublishing.com.

First Edition

Britannica Educational Publishing
J.E. Luebering: Director, Core Reference Group
Anthony L. Green: Editor, Compton's by Britannica

Rosen Publishing
Hope Lourie Killcoyne: Executive Editor
Christine Poolos: Editor
Nelson Sá: Art Director
Michael Moy: Designer
Cindy Reiman: Photography Manager

Introduction and supplementary material by Gina Hagler.

Library of Congress Cataloging-in-Publication Data

Genetic testing and gene therapy/edited by James Wolfe.
    pages cm.—(The biotechnology revolution)
Includes bibliographical references and index.
ISBN 978-1-62275-572-1 (library bound)
1. Genetic disorders—Juvenile literature. 2. Human chromosome abnormalities—Diagnosis—Juvenile literature. 3. Gene therapy—Juvenile literature. I. Wolfe, James, 1960- editor.
RB155.8.G474 2016
616.042—dc23

2014046341

Manufactured in the United States of America

Photo credits: Cover, p. 1 Alex011973/Shutterstock.com; p. xi Leslie Holzer/Science Source/Getty Images; pp. 3, 5, 18, 21, 35, 40, 42, 109, 112, 122 Encyclopædia Britannica, Inc. p. 53 A. Barrington Brown/Science Source; pp. 25, 88 Biophoto Associates/Science Source/Getty Images; pp. 44-45 Monica Schroeder/Science Source; p. 60 sodapix/Getty Images; p. 71 © Phanie/Alamy; p. 74 Ariel Skelley/Blend Images/Getty Images; p. 79 Bruce Dale/National Geographic Image Collection/Getty Images; p. 85 BSIP/UIG/Getty Images; p. 90 Dr. Dominik Refardt/University of Basel, Switzerland.; p. 98 Courtesy of the National Library of Medicine; p. 102 Stocktrek Images/Getty Images; p. 116 Rob Atkins/Photographer's Choice RF/Getty Images; p. 130 DEA/G.Dagli Orti/De Agostini/Getty Images; p. 135 Courtesy Everett Collection; p. 141 Mandel Ngan/AFP/Getty Images; p. 143 Darren Hauck/Getty Images; p. 148 Jeff Kowalsky/AFP/Getty Images; p. 150 Hulton Archive/Getty Images; cover and interior design elements vitstudio/Shutterstock.com (DNA), everythingpossible/iStock/Thinkstock (honeycomb), style_TTT/Shutterstock.com (linear patterns).

CONTENTS

INTRODUCTION VIII

CHAPTER 1
GENES AND HEREDITY 1
CHROMOSOMES AND GENES 2
THE BEHAVIOUR OF CHROMOSOMES DURING CELL DIVISION 3
LINKAGE OF TRAITS 6
CHROMOSOMAL ABERRATIONS 8
MOLECULAR GENETICS 10
DNA AS THE AGENT OF HEREDITY 11
STRUCTURE AND COMPOSITION OF DNA 11
ROSALIND FRANKLIN AND MAURICE WILKINS . . 14
THE GENETIC CODE 16
GENE MUTATION 19

CHAPTER 2
HUMAN GENETIC DISEASE 23
CLASSES OF GENETIC DISEASE 24
DISEASES CAUSED BY CHROMOSOMAL ABERRATIONS . . . 25
NUMERICAL ABNORMALITIES 26
KLINEFELTER SYNDROME 32
DISEASES ASSOCIATED WITH SINGLE-GENE MENDELIAN INHERITANCE 34
DISEASES ASSOCIATED WITH SINGLE-GENE NON-MENDELIAN INHERITANCE 43
DISEASES CAUSED BY MULTIFACTORAL INHERITANCE . 48
GENETICS OF CANCER 49
COGNITIVE AND BEHAVIORAL GENETICS 54

GENETIC DAMAGE FROM ENVIRONMENTAL AGENTS . . . 55
- VIRUSES 56
- PLANTS, FUNGI, AND BACTERIA 57
- INDUSTRIAL CHEMICALS 58
- COMBUSTION PRODUCTS 59
- ALCOHOL 61
- ULTRAVIOLET RADIATION 62
- IONIZING RADIATION 63
- MOLECULAR OXYGEN 64

CHAPTER 3
GENETIC COUNSELING AND TESTING 67
- COUNSELING TO ASSESS GENETIC RISK 70
  - PRENATAL 71
  - INFANCY 75
  - *Testing for Genetic Mutations* 76
  - ADULTHOOD 78
- TYPES OF DIAGNOSTIC GENETIC TESTS 80
- TESTING FOR PRENATAL DIAGNOSIS 81
  - KAROTYPING 87
  - DNA TESTS 89
  - *Genetic Testing and Genealogy* 91
  - BIOCHEMICAL TESTS 92
- TESTING FOR DIAGNOSIS AFTER
  THE NEONATAL PERIOD 92

CHAPTER 4
GENE THERAPY 96

MAPPING THE HUMAN GENOME	97
PREREQUISITES FOR GENE THERAPY	99
Regulation of Gene Therapy Clinical Trials	100
NANOTECHNOLOGY RESEARCH	101
RECOMBINANT DNA TECHNOLOGY	106
DNA CLONING	107
Creating the Clone	108
Vectors	113
Isolating the Clone	114
Reverse Genetics	115
DIAGNOSTICS	115
GENOMICS	117
PROTEIN MANUFACTURE	117
A NEW APPROACH	119
Gene Doping	120
SOMATIC CELL NUCLEAR TRANSFER	121
INDUCED PLURIPOTENT STEM CELLS	124

CHAPTER 5

BIOETHICAL CONSIDERATIONS 128

BIOETHICS	129
The Hippocratic Oath	133
ISSUES IN BIOETHICS	134
THE HEALTH CARE CONTEXT	138
TRADITIONAL PHILOSOPHICAL QUESTIONS	139
SOCIAL AND LEGAL ISSUES	143
TRADITIONAL AND CONTEMPORARY ETHICAL THEORIES	149

    SAVIOUR SIBLINGS................................150
THE FOUR-PRINCIPLES APPROACH..........153
THE SIGNIFICANCE OF PUBLIC ATTITUDES.....155
POLICY MAKING.................................156
GLOBAL BIOETHICS..............................157
    CONCLUSION..................................159
    GLOSSARY....................................160
    BIBLIOGRAPHY................................163
    INDEX..170

INTRODUCTION

Biotechnology is the manipulation of biology or biological/organic processes to make products. Since the 1970s, biotechnology research has focused on the areas of health care, energy/industry, and agriculture. It has produced such remarkable advances as a viral pacemaker, prosthetic limbs that provide feedback, and a rocket-powered arm. It has made it possible to manipulate an individual's DNA. In this volume on genetic testing and gene therapy, the reader will gain an in-depth look at the history, methodologies, processes, applications, and potential for growth in this fascinating field.

THE BIRTH OF GENETICS

Genetics is the study of heredity and genes specifically. Heredity is the sum of all biological processes by which particular characteristics are transmitted from parents to their offspring. The concept of heredity encompasses two seemingly paradoxical observations about organisms: the constancy of a species from generation to generation and the variation among individuals within a species. Constancy and variation are actually two sides of the same coin, as becomes clear in the study of genetics.

INTRODUCTION

Both aspects of heredity can be explained by genes, the functional units of heritable material that are found within all living cells. Every member of a species has a set of genes specific to that species. It is this set of genes that provides the constancy of the species. Among individuals within a species, however, variations can occur in the form each gene takes, providing the genetic basis for the fact that no two individuals (except identical twins) have exactly the same traits.

Heredity was for a long time one of the most puzzling and mysterious phenomena of nature. This was so because the sex cells, which form the bridge across which heredity must pass between the generations, are usually invisible to the naked eye. Only after the invention of the microscope early in the 17th century and the subsequent discovery of the sex cells could the essentials of heredity be grasped. The Greek philosophers, for example, believed that the traits of individuals were acquired from contact with the environment and that such acquired characteristics could be inherited by offspring. Because Lamarck was the most famous proponent of the inheritance of acquired characteristics, the theory is called Lamarckism. This concept, which emphasized the use and disuse of organs as the significant factor in determining the characteristics of an individual, postulated that any alterations in the individual could be transmitted to the offspring through the gametes. Yet the inheritance of acquired characteristics has never been experimentally verified, despite many attempts. Furthermore, many of Lamarck's examples, such as the long neck of the giraffe, can be more satisfactorily explained by means of natural selection.

In 1885 Weismann suggested that hereditary characteristics were transmitted by what he called germ plasm—as distinguished from the somatoplasm (body cells)—which linked the generations by a continuous stream of dividing germ cells. In stating definitely seven years later that the material of heredity was in the chromosomes, Weismann anticipated the chromosomal basis of inheritance.

Francis Galton, a 19th-century English anthropologist, made a number of important contributions to genetics, one of which was a study of the hereditary nature of ability, from which he developed the concept that judicious breeding could improve the human race (eugenics). Galton's most significant work was the demonstration that each generation of ancestors makes a proportionate contribution to the total makeup of the individual. Thus, he suggested that if a tall man marries a short woman, each should contribute half of the total heritage, and the resultant offspring should be intermediate between the two parents.

INTRODUCTION

In 1854, Austrian Augustinian monk Gregor Mendel began a series of experiments that were part of a major experimental program in hybridization at the monastery. The aim of this program was

Gregor Mendel, 1865.

to trace the transmission of hereditary characters in successive generations of hybrid progeny. Previous authorities had observed that progeny of fertile hybrids tended to revert to the originating species, and they had therefore concluded that hybridization could not be a mechanism used by nature to multiply species—though in exceptional cases some fertile hybrids did appear not to revert (the so-called "constant hybrids"). On the other hand, plant and animal breeders had long shown that crossbreeding could indeed produce a multitude of new forms. The latter point was of particular interest to landowners, including the abbot of the monastery, who was concerned about the monastery's future profits from the wool of its Merino sheep, owing to competing wool being supplied from Australia.

Mendel chose to conduct his studies with the edible pea (*Pisum sativum*) because of the numerous distinct varieties, the ease of culture and control of pollination, and the high proportion of successful seed germinations. From 1854 to 1856 he tested 34 varieties for constancy of their traits. In order to trace the transmission of characters, he chose seven traits that were expressed in a distinctive manner, such as plant height (short or tall) and seed colour (green or yellow). He referred to these alternatives as contrasted characters, or character-pairs. He crossed varieties that differed in one trait—for instance, tall crossed with short. The first generation of hybrids (F1) displayed the character of one variety but not that of the other. In Mendel's terms, one character was dominant and the other recessive. In the numerous progeny that he raised from these hybrids (the second generation, F2), however, the recessive character reappeared, and the proportion of offspring bearing the dominant to offspring bearing the recessive was very close to a 3 to 1 ratio. Study of the descendants (F3) of the dominant group showed that one-third of them were true-breeding and two-thirds were of hybrid constitution. The 3:1 ratio could hence be rewritten as 1:2:1, meaning that 50 percent of the F2 generation were true-breeding and 50 percent were still hybrid. This was Mendel's major discovery, and it was unlikely to have been made by his predecessors, since they did not grow statistically significant populations, nor did they follow the individual characters separately to establish their statistical relations.

Mendel's approach to experimentation came from his training in physics and mathematics, especially combinatorial mathematics. The latter served him ideally to represent his result. If A represents the dominant characteristic and a the recessive, then the 1:2:1 ratio recalls the terms in the expansion of the binomial equation:

$$(A + a)2 = A2 + 2Aa + a2$$

Mendel realized further that he could test his expectation that the seven traits are transmitted independently of one another. Crosses involving first two and then three of his seven traits yielded categories of offspring in proportions following the terms produced from combining two binomial equations, indicating that their transmission was independent of one another. Mendel's successors have called this conclusion the law of independent assortment.

Mendel went on to relate his results to the cell theory of fertilization, according to which a new organism is generated from the fusion of two cells. In order for pure breeding forms of both the dominant and the recessive type to be brought into the hybrid, there had to be some temporary accommodation of the two differing characters in the hybrid as well as a separation process in the formation of the pollen cells and the egg cells. In other words, the hybrid must form germ cells bearing the potential to yield either the one characteristic or the other. This has since been described as the law of segregation, or the doctrine of the purity of the germ cells. Since one pollen cell fuses with one egg cell, all possible combinations of the differing pollen and egg cells would yield just the results suggested by Mendel's combinatorial theory.

Mendel first presented his results in two separate lectures in 1865 to the Natural Science Society in

Brünn. His paper "Experiments on Plant Hybrids" was published in the society's journal, *Verhandlungen des naturforschenden Vereines in Brünn*, the following year. It attracted little attention, although many libraries received it and reprints were sent out. The tendency of those who read it was to conclude that Mendel had simply demonstrated more accurately what was already widely assumed—namely, that hybrid progeny revert to their originating forms. They overlooked the potential for variability and the evolutionary implications that his demonstration of the recombination of traits made possible. Most notably, Swiss botanist Karl Wilhelm von Nägeli actually corresponded with Mendel, despite remaining skeptical as to the significance of his results and doubting that the germ cells in hybrids could be pure. Mendel appears to have made no effort to publicize his work, and it is not known how many reprints of his paper he distributed.

In 1900 Dutch botanist and geneticist Hugo de Vries, German botanist and geneticist Carl Erich Correns, and Austrian botanist Erich Tschermak von Seysenegg independently reported results of hybridization experiments similar to Mendel's, though each later claimed not to have known of Mendel's work while doing their own experiments. However, both de Vries and Correns had read Mendel earlier—Correns even made detailed notes on the subject—but had forgotten. De Vries had a diversity of results in 1899, but it was not until he reread Mendel in 1900 that he was able to select and organize his data into a rational system. Tschermak had not read Mendel before obtaining his results, and his first account of his data offers an interpretation in terms of hereditary potency. He described the 3:1 ratio as an "unequal valancy" (*Wertigkeit*). In subsequent papers he incorporated the Mendelian theory of segregation and the purity of the germ cells into his text.

UNIVERSALITY OF MENDEL'S LAWS

Although Mendel experimented with varieties of peas, his laws have been shown to apply to the inheritance of many kinds of characters in almost all organisms. In 1902 Mendelian inheritance was demonstrated in poultry (by English geneticists William Bateson and Reginald Punnett) and in mice. The following year, albinism became the first human trait shown to be a Mendelian recessive, with pigmented skin the corresponding dominant.

In 1902 and 1909, English physician Sir Archibald Garrod initiated the analysis of inborn errors of metabolism in humans in terms of biochemical genetics. Alkaptonuria, inherited as a recessive, is characterized by excretion in the urine of large amounts of the substance called alkapton, or homogentisic acid, which renders the urine black on exposure to air. In normal (i.e., nonalkaptonuric) persons the homogentisic acid is changed to acetoacetic acid, the reaction being facilitated by an enzyme, homogentisic acid oxidase. Garrod advanced the hypothesis that this enzyme is absent or inactive in homozygous carriers of the defective recessive alkaptonuria gene; hence, the homogentisic acid accumulates and is excreted in the urine. Mendelian inheritance of numerous traits in humans has been studied since then.

The distinction between a characteristic and its determinant was not consistently made by Mendel or by his successors, the early Mendelians. In 1909 Danish botanist and geneticist Wilhelm Johannsen clarified this point and named the determinants genes. Four years later American zoologist and geneticist Thomas Hunt Morgan located the genes on the chromosomes, and the popular picture of them as beads on a string emerged. This discovery had implications for Mendel's claim of an independent transmission of traits, for genes close together on the same chromosome are not transmitted independently. Moreover, as genetic studies pushed the analysis down to smaller and smaller dimensions, the Mendelian gene appeared to fragment. Molecular genetics has thus challenged any attempts to achieve a unified conception of the gene as the elementary unit of heredity. Today the gene is defined in several ways, depending upon the nature of the investigation. Genetic material can be synthesized, manipulated, and hybridized with genetic material from other species, but to fully understand its functions in the whole organism, an understanding of Mendelian inheritance is necessary.

As the architect of genetic experimental and statistical analysis, Mendel remains the acknowledged father of genetics. It is his experimental work with pea plants that set the stage for the developments you will read about in the following chapters.

CHAPTER 1

GENES AND HEREDITY

The set of genes that an offspring inherits from both parents, a combination of the genetic material of each, is called the organism's genotype. The genotype is contrasted to the phenotype, which is the organism's outward appearance and the developmental outcome of its genes. The phenotype includes an organism's bodily structures, physiological processes, and behaviours. Although the genotype determines the broad limits of the features an organism can develop, the features that actually develop, i.e., the phenotype, depend on complex interactions between genes and their environment. The genotype remains constant throughout an organism's lifetime; however, because the organism's internal and external environments change continuously, so does its phenotype. In conducting genetic studies, it is crucial to discover the degree to which the observable trait is attributable to the pattern of genes in the cells and to what extent it arises from environmental influence.

CHROMOSOMES AND GENES

Each individual in a sexually reproducing species inherits two alleles for each gene, one from each parent. Furthermore, when such an individual forms sex cells, each of the resultant gametes receives one member of each allelic pair. The formation of gametes occurs through a process of cell division called meiosis. When gametes unite in fertilization, the double dose of hereditary material is restored, and a new individual is created. This individual, consisting at first of only one cell, grows via mitosis, a process of repeated cell divisions. Mitosis differs from meiosis in that each daughter cell receives a full copy of all the hereditary material found in the parent cell.

It is apparent that the genes must physically reside in cellular structures that meet two criteria. First, these structures must be replicated and passed on to each generation of daughter cells during mitosis. Second, they must be organized into homologous pairs, one member of which is parceled out to each gamete formed during meiosis. During mitosis, cell nuclei resolve themselves into small rodlike bodies called chromosomes. Chromosomes are the carriers of genes.

GENES AND HEREDITY

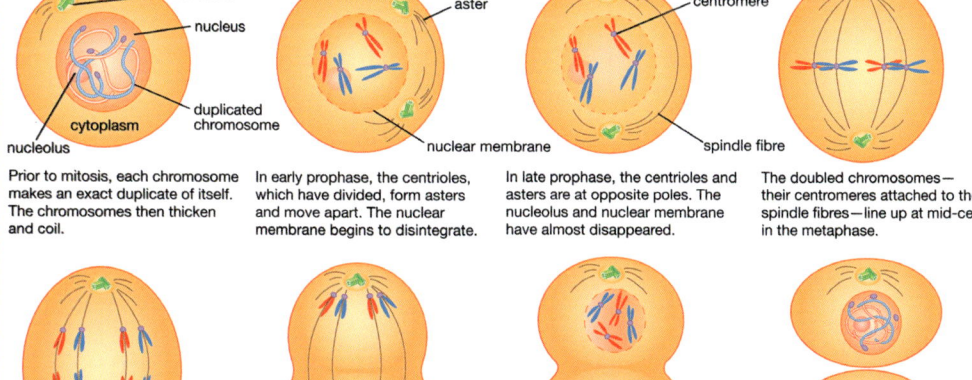

One cell gives rise to two genetically identical daughter cells during the process of mitosis.

THE BEHAVIOUR OF CHROMOSOMES DURING CELL DIVISION

When the chromosomes condense during cell division, they have already undergone replication. Each chromosome thus consists of two identical replicas, called chromatids, joined at a point called the centromere. During mitosis the sister chromatids separate, one going to each daughter cell. Chromosomes thus meet the first criterion for being the repository of genes: they are replicated, and a full copy is passed to each daughter cell during mitosis.

The number of chromosomes within the nucleus is usually constant in all individuals of a given species — for example, 46 in the human. In sexually reproducing organisms, this number is called the diploid number of chromosomes, as it represents the double dose of chromosomes received from two parents. The nucleus of a gamete, however, contains half this number of chromosomes, or the haploid number. Thus, a human gamete contains 23 chromosomes. Meiosis produces the haploid gametes.

The essential features of meiosis are shown in the diagram. For the sake of simplicity, the diploid parent cell is shown to contain a single pair of homologous chromosomes, one member of which is represented in blue (from the father) and the other in red (from the mother). At the leptotene stage the chromosomes appear as long, thin threads. At pachytene they pair, the corresponding portions of the two chromosomes lying side by side. The chromosomes then duplicate and contract into paired chromatids. At this stage the pair of chromosomes is known as a tetrad, as it consists of four chromatids. Also at this stage an extremely important event occurs: portions of the maternal and paternal chromosomes are exchanged. This exchange process, called crossing over, results in chromatids

GENES AND HEREDITY

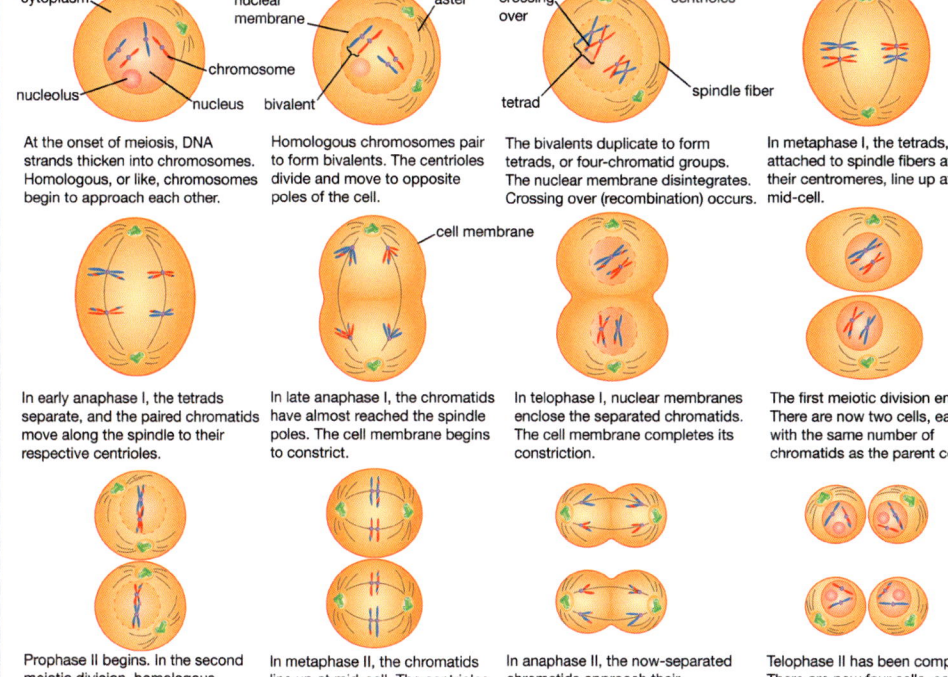

The formation of gametes (sex cells) occurs during the process of meiosis.

that include both paternal and maternal genes and consequently introduces new genetic combinations. The first meiotic division separates the chromosomal tetrads, with the paternal chromosome (whose chromatids now contain some maternal genes) going to one cell and the maternal chromosome (containing some paternal genes) going to another cell. During the second meiotic division the chromatids separate. The original diploid cell has thus given rise to four haploid gametes (only two of which are shown in the diagram). Not only has a reduction in chromosome number occurred, but the resulting single member of each homologous chromosome pair may be a new combination (through crossing over) of genes present in the original diploid cell.

LINKAGE OF TRAITS

The random assortment of the maternal and paternal chromosomes at meiosis is the physical basis of the independent assortment of genes and of the traits they control. The number of the genes in a sex cell is, however, much greater than that of the chromosomes. When two or more genes are borne on the same chromosome, these genes may not be assorted independently; such genes are said to be linked.

The linkage maps of the chromosomes are really summaries of many statistical observations on the outcomes of hybridization experiments. In principle at least, such maps could be prepared even if the chromosomes, not to speak of the chiasmata at meiosis, were unknown. In most organisms, including humans, chiasmata are seen in the meiotic chromosomes in both sexes, and observations on hybrid progenies show that recombination of linked genes occurs also in both sexes.

The male of many animals has one chromosome pair, the sex chromosomes, consisting of unequal members called X and Y. At meiosis the X and Y chromosomes first pair then disjoin and pass to different cells. One-half of the gametes (spermatozoa) formed contain the X chromosome and the other half the Y. The female has two X chromosomes; all egg cells normally carry a single X. The eggs fertilized by X-bearing spermatozoa give females (XX), and those fertilized by Y-bearing spermatozoa give males (XY).

The genes located in the X chromosomes exhibit what is known as sex-linkage or crisscross inheritance. This is because of a crucial difference between the paired sex chromosomes and the other pairs of chromosomes (called autosomes). The members of the autosome pairs are truly homologous; that is, each member of a pair contains a full complement of the same genes (albeit, perhaps, in different allelic forms). The sex chromosomes, on the other hand, do not constitute a homologous pair, as the X chromosome is much larger and carries far more genes than does the Y. Consequently, many recessive alleles carried on the X chromosome of a male will be expressed just as if they were dominant, for the Y chromosome carries no genes to counteract them. In humans, red-green colour blindness and hemophilia are among many traits showing sex linked inheritance and are consequently due to genes borne in the X chromosome.

CHROMOSOMAL ABERRATIONS

The chromosome set of a species remains relatively stable over long periods of time. However, within populations there can be found abnormalities involving the structure or number of chromosomes. These alterations arise spontaneously from errors in the normal processes of the cell. Their consequences are usually deleterious, giving rise to individuals who are unhealthy or sterile, though in rare cases alterations provide new adaptive opportunities that allow evolutionary change to occur. In fact, the discovery of visible chromosomal differences between species has given rise to the belief that radical restructuring of chromosome architecture has been an important force in evolution.

CHANGES IN CHROMOSOME STRUCTURE

Two important principles dictate the properties of a large proportion of structural chromosomal changes. The first principle is that any deviation from the normal ratio of genetic material in the genome results in genetic imbalance and abnormal function. In the normal nuclei of both diploid and haploid cells, the ratio of the individual chromosomes to one another is 1:1. Any deviation from this ratio by addition or subtraction of either whole chromosomes or parts of chromosomes results in genomic imbalance. The second principle is that homologous chromosomes go to great lengths to pair at meiosis. The tightly paired homologous regions are joined by a ladderlike longitudinal structure called the synaptonemal complex. Homologous regions seem to be able to find each other and form a synaptonemal complex whether or not they are part of normal chromosomes. Therefore, when structural changes occur, not only are the resulting pairing formations highly characteristic of that type of structural change but they also dictate the packaging of normal and abnormal chromosomes into the gametes and subsequently into the progeny.

The simplest, but perhaps most damaging, structural change is a deletion—the complete loss of a part of one chromosome. In a haploid cell this is lethal, because part of the essential genome is lost. However, even in diploid cells deletions are generally lethal or have other serious consequences. In a diploid a heterozygous deletion results in a cell that has one normal chromosome set and another set that contains a truncated chromosome. Such cells show genomic imbalance, which increases in severity with the size of the deletion. Another potential source of damage is that any recessive, deleterious, or lethal alleles that are in the normal counterpart of the deleted region will be expressed in the phenotype. In humans, cri-du-chat syndrome is caused by a heterozygous deletion at the tip of the short arm of chromosome 5. Infants are born with this condition as the result of a deletion arising in parental germinal tissues or even in sex cells. The manifestations of this deletion, in addition to the "cat cry" that gives the syndrome its name, include severe intellectual disability and an abnormally small head.

A heterozygous duplication (an extra copy of some chromosome region) also results in a genomic imbalance with deleterious consequences. Small duplications within a gene can arise spontaneously. Larger duplications can be caused by crossovers following asymmetrical chromosome pairing or by meiotic irregularities resulting from other types of altered chromosome structures. If a duplication becomes homozygous, it can provide the organism with an opportunity to acquire new genetic functions through mutations within the duplicate copy.

MOLECULAR GENETICS

The data accumulated by scientists of the early 20th century provided compelling evidence that chromosomes are the carriers of genes. But the nature of the genes themselves remained a mystery, as did the mechanism by which they exert their influence. Molecular genetics—the study of the structure and function of genes at the molecular level—provided answers to these fundamental questions.

DNA AS THE AGENT OF HEREDITY

In 1869 Swiss chemist Johann Friedrich Miescher extracted deoxyribonucleic acid, or DNA, from cell nuclei. DNA is the chemical component of the chromosomes that is chiefly responsible for their staining properties in microscopic preparations. Today the genetic makeup of most organisms can be transformed using externally applied DNA. Transforming DNA is able to pass through cellular and nuclear membranes and then integrate into the chromosomal DNA of the recipient cell. Furthermore, using modern DNA technology, it is possible to isolate the section of chromosomal DNA that constitutes an individual gene, manipulate its structure, and reintroduce it into a cell to cause changes that show beyond doubt that the DNA is responsible for a large part of the overall characteristics of an organism. For reasons such as these, it is now accepted that, in all living organisms, with the exception of some viruses, genes are composed of DNA.

STRUCTURE AND COMPOSITION OF DNA

Nucleic acids are long chainlike molecules, the backbones of which consist of repeated sequences of phosphate and sugar linkages—ribose sugar in RNA and deoxyribose sugar in DNA. Attached to the sugar links in the backbone are two kinds of nitrogenous bases: purines and pyrimidines. The purines are adenine (A) and guanine (G) in both DNA and RNA; the pyrimidines are cytosine (C) and thymine (T) in DNA and cytosine (C) and uracil (U) in RNA. A single purine or pyrimidine is attached to each sugar, and the entire phosphate-sugar-base subunit is called a nucleotide. The nucleic acids extracted from different species of animals and plants have different proportions of the four nucleotides. Some are relatively richer in adenine and thymine, while others have more guanine and cytosine. However, it was found by biochemist Erwin Chargaff that the amount of A is always equal to T, and the amount of G is always equal to C.

The structure of DNA was determined by American geneticist James Watson and British biophysicist Francis Crick in 1953. The pair devised their now-famous model showing DNA as a double helix composed of two intertwined chains of nucleotides, in which the adenines of one chain are linked to the thymines of the other, and the guanines in one chain are linked to the cytosines of the other. The structure resembles a ladder that has been twisted into a spiral shape: the sides of the ladder are composed of sugar and phosphate groups, and the rungs are made up of the paired nitrogenous bases. By making a wire model of the structure, it became clear that the only way the model could conform to the requirements of the molecular

GENES AND HEREDITY

Francis Crick and James Watson, along with their team, determined the structure of DNA.

ROSALIND FRANKLIN AND MAURICE WILKINS

Watson and Crick are the names most often associated with the discovery of DNA, but in fact there was an entire team of scientists responsible for the monumental advance. Among them were Rosalind Franklin and Maurice Wilkins. Indeed, Wilkins shared the 1962 Nobel Prize for Physiology or Medicine with Crick and Watson, but many scientists believed that Franklin should have been honored with them.

Born in London on July 25, 1920, Franklin won a scholarship to Newnham College, Cambridge. After graduation in 1941 she began research on the physical structure of coals and carbonized coals. Working in Paris from 1947 to 1950, she gained skill in using X-ray diffraction as an analytical technique. Franklin used this technique to describe the structure of carbons with more precision than had previously been possible. She also determined that there are two distinct classes of carbons—those that form graphite when they are heated to high temperatures and those that do not.

In 1951 Franklin joined the King's College Medical Research Council biophysics unit. With Raymond Gosling she conducted X-ray diffraction studies of the molecular structure of DNA. Based on these studies, she first concluded that the structure was helical (having spiral arms). Later research caused her to change her mind, and it was left to Watson and Crick to develop the double-helix model of the molecule that proved to be consistent with DNA's known properties. Some of the data used by those scientists in their successful effort, however, was first produced by Franklin.

From 1953 until her death on April 16, 1958, Franklin worked at the crystallography laboratory of Birkbeck College, London. There she published her earlier work on coals and helped determine the structure of the tobacco mosaic virus.

The son of a physician, Wilkins was born in 1916 and educated at King Edward's School in Birmingham, England, and St. John's College, Cambridge. He participated for two years during World War II in the Manhattan Project at the University of California, Berkeley, working on mass spectrograph separation of uranium isotopes for use in the atomic bomb.

Upon his return to Great Britain, Wilkins lectured at the University of St. Andrews in Scotland. In 1946 he joined the Medical Research Council's Biophysics Unit at King's College in London. In 1955 he became its deputy director, and from 1970 to 1980 he served as the unit's director. There he began the series of investigations that led ultimately to his X-ray diffraction studies of DNA. Wilkins headed a group that included Franklin. Wilkins later applied X-ray diffraction techniques to the study of ribonucleic acid.

At King's College proper, Wilkins was professor of molecular biology (1963–70) and of biophysics (1970–81) and emeritus professor thereafter. While there he published literature on light microscopy techniques for cytochemical research. His autobiography, *The Third Man of the Double Helix*, was published in 2003.

dimensions of DNA was if A always paired with T and G with C; in fact, the A-T and G-C pairs showed a satisfying lock-and-key fit. Although most of the bonds in DNA are strong covalent bonds, the A-T and G-C bonds are weak hydrogen bonds. However, multiple hydrogen bonds along the centre of the molecule confer enough stability to hold the two strands together.

Watson and Crick noted that their proposed DNA structure fulfilled two necessary features of a hereditary molecule. First, a hereditary molecule must be capable of replication so that the information can be passed on to the next generation; therefore, Watson and Crick hypothesized that, if the two halves of the double helix could separate, they could act as templates for the synthesis of two identical double helices. Second, a hereditary molecule must contain information to guide the development of a complete organism; therefore, Watson and Crick speculated that the sequence of nucleotides might represent coded information of this sort. Subsequent research showed that their speculations on both points were correct.

THE GENETIC CODE

Hereditary information is contained in the nucleotide sequence of DNA in a kind of code. The coded information is copied faithfully into RNA and translated into chains of amino acids. Amino acid chains are folded into helices, zigzags, and other shapes and are sometimes associated with other amino acid chains. The specific amounts of amino acids in a protein and their sequence determine the protein's unique properties; for example, muscle protein and hair protein contain the same 20 amino acids, but the sequences of these amino acids in the two proteins are quite different. If the nucleotide sequence of mRNA is thought of as a written message, it can be said that this message is read by the translation apparatus in "words" of three nucleotides, starting at one end of the mRNA and proceeding along the length of the molecule. These three-letter words are called codons. Each codon stands for a specific amino acid, so if the message in mRNA is 900 nucleotides long, which corresponds to 300 codons, it will be translated into a chain of 300 amino acids. Each of the three letters in a codon can be filled by any one of the four nucleotides; therefore, there are 4^3, or 64, possible codons. Each one of these 64 words in the codon dictionary has meaning.

One of the surprising findings about the genetic codon dictionary is that, with a few exceptions, it is the same in all organisms. (One exception is mitochondrial DNA, which exhibits several differences from the standard genetic code and also between organisms.) The uniformity of the genetic code has been interpreted as an indication of the evolutionary relatedness of all organisms. For the purpose of genetic research, codon uniformity is convenient

Semiconservative DNA replication

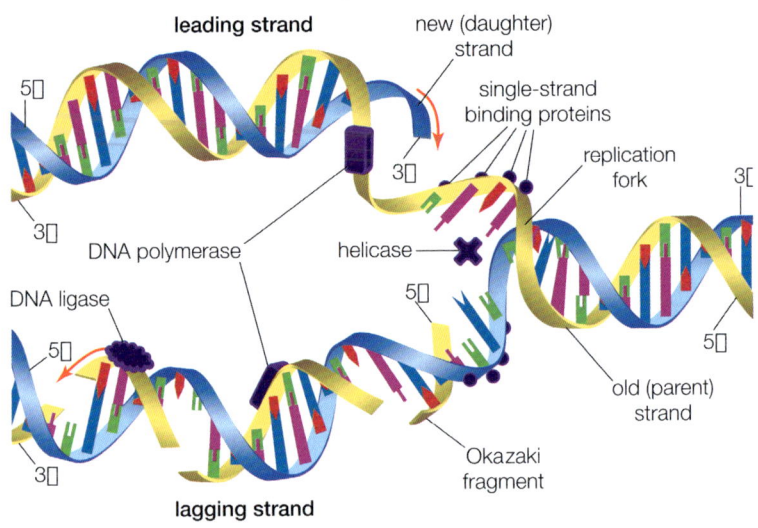

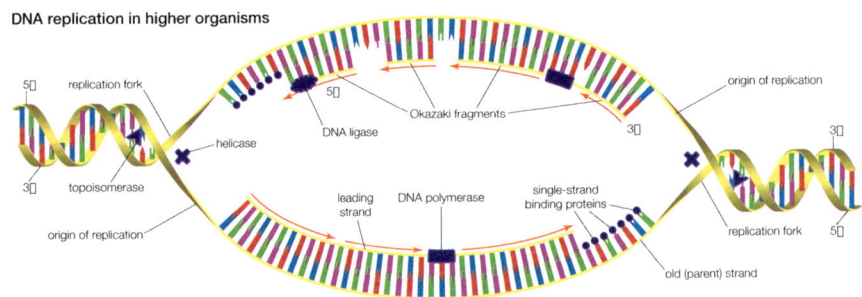

In semiconservative DNA replication (top) an existing DNA molecule is separated into two template strands. New nucleotides align with and bind to the nucleotides of the existing strands, thus forming two DNA molecules that are identical to the original DNA molecule. DNA replication in higher organisms (bottom) begins at multiple origins of replication and progresses in two directions.

because any type of DNA can be translated in any organism.

GENE MUTATION

Given the complexity of DNA and the vast number of cell divisions that take place within the lifetime of a multicellular organism, copying errors are likely to occur. If unrepaired, such errors will change the sequence of the DNA bases and alter the genetic code. Mutation is the random process whereby genes change from one allelic form to another. Scientists who study mutation use the most common genotype found in natural populations, called the wild type, as the standard against which to compare a mutant allele. Mutation can occur in two directions; mutation from wild type to mutant is called a forward mutation, and mutation from mutant to wild type is called a back mutation or reversion.

Mutations arise from changes to the DNA of a gene. These changes can be quite small, affecting only one nucleotide pair, or they can be relatively large, affecting hundreds or thousands of nucleotides. Mutations can affect gene function in several different ways. First, the structure and function of the protein coded by that gene can be affected. For example, enzymes are particularly susceptible to mutations that affect the amino acid sequence at their active site (i.e., the region that allows the enzyme to bind with its specific substrate). This may lead to enzyme inactivity; a protein is made, but it has no enzymatic function. Second, some nonsense or frameshift mutations can lead to the complete absence of a protein. Third, changes to the promoter region of the gene can result in gene malfunction by interfering with transcription. In this situation, protein production is either inhibited or it occurs at an inappropriate time because of alterations somewhere in the regulatory region. Fourth, mutations within introns that affect the specific nucleotide sequences that direct intron splicing may result in an mRNA that still contains an intron. When translated, this extra RNA will almost certainly be meaningless at the protein level, and its extra length will lead to a functionless protein. Any mutation that results in a lack of function for a particular gene is called a "null" mutation. Less-severe mutations are called "leaky" mutations because some normal function still "leaks through" into the phenotype.

Most mutations occur spontaneously and have no known cause. The synthesis of DNA is a cooperative venture of many different interacting cellular components, and occasionally mistakes occur that result in mutations. Like many chemical structures, the bases of DNA are able to exist in several conformations called isomers. The keto form of a DNA base is the normal form that gives the molecule

GENES AND HEREDITY

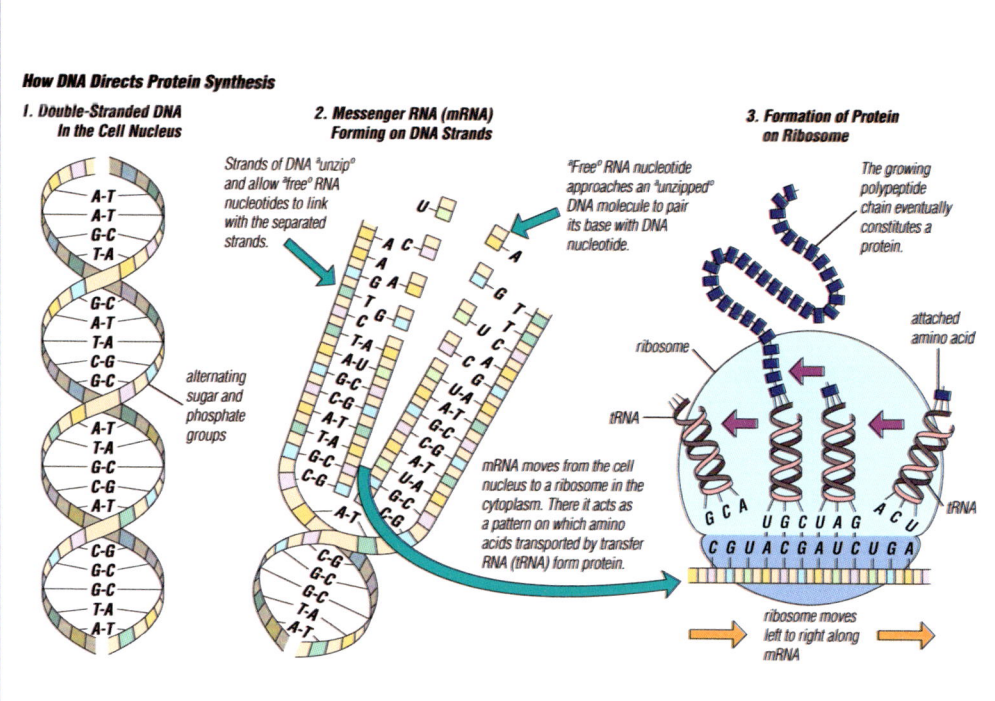

DNA in the cell nucleus carries a genetic code. Messenger RNA (mRNA) then travels to the ribosomes in the cell cytoplasm, where protein synthesis occurs. Finally, the synthesized protein is released to perform its task in the cell or elsewhere in the body.

its standard base-pairing properties. However, the keto form occasionally changes spontaneously to the enol form, which has different base-pairing properties. For example, the keto form of cytosine pairs with guanine (its normal pairing partner), but the enol form of cytosine pairs with adenine. During

DNA replication, this adenine base will act as the template for thymine in the newly synthesized strand. Therefore, a CG base pair will have mutated to a TA base pair. If this change results in a functionally different amino acid, then a missense mutation may result. Another spontaneous event that can lead to mutation is depurination, the complete loss of a purine base (adenine or guanine) at some location in the DNA. The resulting gap can be filled by any base during subsequent replications.

Researchers have demonstrated that ionizing radiation, some chemicals, and certain viruses are capable of acting as mutagens—agents that can increase the rate at which mutations occur. Some mutagens have been implicated as a cause of cancer. For example, ultraviolet (UV) radiation from the sun is known to cause skin cancer, and cigarette smoke is a primary cause of lung cancer.

CHAPTER 2

HUMAN GENETIC DISEASE

With the increasing ability to control infectious and nutritional diseases in developed countries, there has come the realization that genetic diseases—any of the diseases and disorders that are caused by mutations in one or more genes—are a major cause of disability, death, and human tragedy. Rare, indeed, is the family that is entirely free of any known genetic disorder. Many thousands of different genetic disorders with defined clinical symptoms have been identified. Of the 3 to 6 percent of newborns with a recognized birth defect, at least half involve a predominantly genetic contribution. Furthermore, genetic defects are the major known cause of pregnancy loss in developed nations, and almost half of all spontaneous abortions (miscarriages) involve a chromosomally abnormal fetus. About 30 percent of all postnatal infant mortality in developed countries is due to genetic disease; 30 percent of pediatric and 10 percent of adult hospital admissions can be traced to a predominantly genetic cause. Finally, medical investigators estimate that genetic defects—however minor—are present in at least 10 percent of all adults. Thus, these are not rare events.

A congenital defect is any biochemical, functional, or structural abnormality that originates prior to or shortly after birth. It must be emphasized that birth defects do not all have the same basis, and it is even possible for apparently identical defects in different individuals to reflect different underlying causes. Though the genetic and biochemical bases for most recognized defects are still uncertain, it is evident that many of these disorders result from a combination of genetic and environmental factors.

CLASSES OF GENETIC DISEASE

Most human genetic defects can be categorized as resulting from either chromosomal, single-gene Mendelian, single-gene non-Mendelian, or multifactorial causes. Each of these categories is discussed briefly below.

HUMAN GENETIC DISEASE

DISEASES CAUSED BY CHROMOSOMAL ABERRATIONS

About 1 out of 150 live newborns has a detectable chromosomal abnormality. Yet even this high incidence represents only a small fraction of chromosome mutations since the vast majority are lethal and result in prenatal death or stillbirth. Indeed, 50 percent of all first-trimester miscarriages and 20 percent of all second-trimester miscarriages are estimated to involve a chromosomally abnormal fetus.

Chromosome disorders can be grouped into three principal categories: (1) those that involve numerical abnormalities of the autosomes, (2) those that involve structural abnormalities of the autosomes, and (3) those that involve the sex chromosomes. Autosomes are the 22 sets of chromosomes found in all normal human cells. They are referred to numerically (e.g., chromosome 1, chromosome 2) according

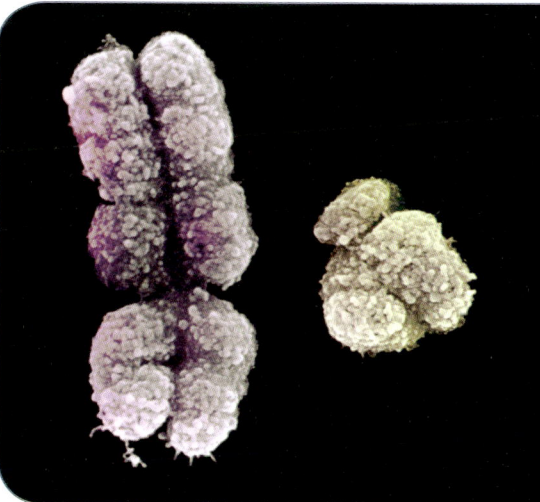

This microscopic image shows an X chromosome and a Y chromosome. The combination of sex chromosomes inherited during fertilization determines a person's sex.

to a traditional sort order based on size, shape, and other properties. Sex chromosomes make up the 23rd pair of chromosomes in all normal human cells and come in two forms, X and Y. In humans and many other animals, it is the constitution of sex chromosomes that determines the sex of the individual, such that XX results in a female and XY results in a male.

NUMERICAL ABNORMALITIES

Numerical abnormalities, involving either the autosomes or sex chromosomes, are believed generally to result from meiotic nondisjunction—that is, the unequal division of chromosomes between daughter cells—that can occur during either maternal or paternal gamete formation. Meiotic nondisjunction leads to eggs or sperm with additional or missing chromosomes. Although the biochemical basis of numerical chromosome abnormalities remains unknown, maternal age clearly has an effect, such that older women are at significantly increased risk to conceive and give birth to a chromosomally abnormal child. The risk increases with age in an almost exponential manner, especially after age 35, so that a pregnant woman age 45 or older has between a 1 in 20 and 1 in 50 chance that her child will have trisomy 21 (Down syndrome), while the risk is only 1 in 400 for a 35-year-old woman and less than 1 in 1,000 for a woman under the age of 30.

There is no clear effect of paternal age on numerical chromosome abnormalities.

Although Down syndrome is probably the best-known and most commonly observed of the autosomal trisomies, being found in about 1 out of 800 live births, both trisomy 13 and trisomy 18 are also seen in the population, albeit at greatly reduced rates (1 out of 10,000 live births and 1 out of 6,000 live births, respectively). The vast majority of conceptions involving trisomy for any of these three autosomes are nonetheless lost to miscarriage, as are all conceptions involving trisomy for any of the other autosomes. Similarly, monosomy for any of the autosomes is lethal in utero and therefore is not seen in the population. Because numerical chromosomal abnormalities generally result from independent meiotic events, parents who have one pregnancy with a numerical chromosomal abnormality are generally not at markedly increased risk above the general population to repeat the experience. Nonetheless, a small increased risk is generally cited for these couples to account for unusual situations, such as chromosomal translocations or gonadal mosaicism.

STRUCTURAL ABNORMALITIES

Structural abnormalities of the autosomes are even more common in the population than are numerical abnormalities and include translocations of large pieces of chromosomes, as well as smaller deletions, insertions, or rearrangements. Indeed, about 5 percent of all cases of Down syndrome result not from classic trisomy 21 but from the presence of excess chromosome 21 material attached to the end of another chromosome as the result of a translocation event. If balanced, structural chromosomal abnormalities may be compatible with a normal phenotype, although unbalanced chromosome structural abnormalities can be every bit as devastating as numerical abnormalities. Furthermore, because many structural defects are inherited from a parent who is a balanced carrier, couples who have one pregnancy with a structural chromosomal abnormality generally are at significantly increased risk above the general population to repeat the experience. Clearly, the likelihood of a recurrence would depend on whether a balanced form of the structural defect occurs in one of the parents.

Even a small deletion or addition of autosomal material—too small to be seen by normal karyotyping methods—can produce serious malformations and intellectual disability. One example is *cri du chat* (French: "cry of the cat") syndrome, which is associated with the loss of a small segment of the short arm of chromosome 5. Newborns with this disorder have a "mewing" cry like that of a cat. Intellectual disability is usually severe.

HUMAN GENETIC DISEASE

ABNORMALITIES OF THE SEX CHROMOSOMES

About 1 in 400 male and 1 in 650 female live births demonstrate some form of sex chromosome abnormality, although the symptoms of these conditions are generally much less severe than are those associated with autosomal abnormalities. Turner syndrome is a condition of females who, in the classic form, carry only a single X chromosome (45,X). Turner syndrome is characterized by a collection of symptoms, including short stature, webbed neck, and incomplete or absent development of secondary sex characteristics, leading to infertility. Although Turner syndrome is seen in about 1 in 2,500 to 1 in 5,000 female live births, the 45,X karyotype accounts for 10 to 20 percent of the chromosomal abnormalities seen in spontaneously aborted fetuses, demonstrating that almost all 45,X conceptions are lost to miscarriage. Indeed, the majority of liveborn females with Turner syndrome are diagnosed as mosaics, meaning that some proportion of their cells are 45,X while the rest are either 46,XX or 46,XY. The degree of clinical severity generally correlates inversely with the degree of mosaicism, so that females with a higher proportion of normal cells will tend to have a milder clinical outcome.

In contrast to Turner syndrome, which results from the absence of a sex chromosome, three alternative conditions result from the presence of an extra sex chromosome: Klinefelter syndrome, trisomy X, and 47,XYY syndrome. These conditions, each of which occurs in about 1 in 1,000 live births, are clinically mild, perhaps reflecting the fact that the Y chromosome carries relatively few genes, and, although the X chromosome is gene-rich, most of these genes become transcriptionally silent in all but one X chromosome in each somatic cell (i.e., all cells except eggs and sperm) via a process called X inactivation. The phenomenon of X inactivation prevents a female who carries two copies of the X chromosome in every cell from expressing twice the amount of gene products encoded exclusively on the X chromosome, in comparison with males, who carry a single X. In brief, at some point in early development one X chromosome in each somatic cell of a female embryo undergoes chemical modification and is inactivated so that gene expression no longer occurs from that template. This process is apparently random in most embryonic tissues, so that roughly half of the cells in each somatic tissue will inactivate the maternal X while the other half will inactivate the paternal X. Cells destined to give rise to eggs do not undergo X inactivation, and cells of the extra-embryonic tissues preferentially inactivate the paternal X, although the rationale for this preference is unclear. The inactivated X chromosome typically replicates later than other chromosomes, and it physically condenses to form a Barr body, a small structure found at the rim of the nucleus in female somatic cells between divisions. The discovery of X inactivation is generally attributed to British geneticist Mary Lyon, and it is therefore often called "lyonization."

The result of X inactivation is that all normal females are mosaics with regard to this chromosome, meaning that they are composed of some cells that express genes only from the maternal X chromosome and others that express genes only from the paternal X chromosome. Although the process is apparently random, not every female has an exact 1:1 ratio of maternal to paternal X inactivation. Indeed, studies suggest that ratios of X inactivation can vary. Furthermore, not all genes on the X chromosome are inactivated; a small number escape modification and remain actively expressed from both X chromosomes in the cell. Although this class of genes has not yet been fully characterized, aberrant expression of these genes has been raised as one possible explanation for the phenotypic abnormalities experienced by individuals with too few or too many X chromosomes.

Klinefelter syndrome (47,XXY) occurs in males and is associated with increased stature and infertility. Gynecomastia (i.e., partial breast development in a male) is sometimes also seen. Males with Klinefelter syndrome, like normal females, inactivate one of their two X chromosomes

KLINEFELTER SYNDROME

Klinefelter syndrome is one of the most frequent chromosomal disorders in males, occurring in approximately 1 in every 500 to 1,000 males. Men with Klinefelter syndrome have small, firm testes, and they often have breast enlargement (gynecomastia) and inordinately long legs and arms (eunuchoidism) and are infertile. Affected men have decreased serum testosterone concentrations, with urinary excretion of 17-ketosteroids (components of certain male hormones, or androgens) in the normal or low-normal range. They also have increased serum follicle-stimulating hormone and luteinizing hormone concentrations. Diabetes mellitus, goitre (enlargement of the thyroid gland), and various cancers may be more prevalent among Klinefelter syndrome patients. Thyroidal trapping of radioactive iodine and the responses of the thyroid to injections of thyrotropin (thyroid-stimulating hormone; TSH) may be low. Although normal in intelligence, some affected men have difficulties making social adjustments.

Klinefelter syndrome is named for Harry Klinefelter, an American physician who in 1942 described a set of symptoms that characterized the condition. The syndrome was first identified with a specific chromosomal abnormality in 1959 by British researcher Patricia A. Jacobs and her colleagues. It results from an unequal sharing of sex chromosomes very soon after fertilization, with one cell of a dividing pair receiving two X chromosomes and a Y chromosome and the other cell of the pair receiving only a Y chromosome and usually dying.

HUMAN GENETIC DISEASE

The normal male chromosome number and sex chromosome composition is 46,XY. However, because males with mosaic (tissues made up of genetically different cells) Klinefelter syndrome have an extra X chromosome, they typically have a chromosome composition of 47,XXY. Men with this form of the disorder usually have fewer symptoms than do men with the other chromosomal arrangements associated with Klinefelter syndrome. Other, rare chromosome complements that give rise to mosaic Klinefelter syndrome include 48,XXYY, 48,XXXY, 49,XXXYY, and 49,XXXXY. Men with these chromosome complements suffer from a variety of additional abnormalities, and, unlike men with 47,XXY Klinefelter syndrome, they often suffer from intellectual disability. One variant of the disorder in particular, the 49,XXXXY type, is characterized by fusion of the forearm bones and other skeletal anomalies, underdevelopment of the penis and scrotum, incomplete descent of the testes, and marked intellectual disability. Although about 40 percent of men affected by Klinefelter syndrome have a normal XY pattern, others possess a chromosome variant known as XX syndrome, in which Y chromosome material is transferred to an X chromosome or a nonsex chromosome (autosome). Men with XX syndrome have a male phenotype (physical appearance), but they have changes typical of Klinefelter syndrome.

Treatment with androgens reduces gynecomastia and evidence of male hypogonadism and increases strength and libido in patients with all variants of Klinefelter syndrome. In a few of these individuals, sperm obtained from the testes have successfully fertilized oocytes in vitro.

in each cell, perhaps explaining, at least in part, the relatively mild clinical outcome.

Trisomy X (47,XXX) is seen in females and is generally also considered clinically benign, although menstrual irregularities or sterility have been noted in some cases. Females with trisomy X inactivate two of the three X chromosomes in each of their cells, again perhaps explaining the clinically benign outcome.

47,XYY syndrome also occurs in males and is associated with tall stature but few, if any, other clinical manifestations. There is some evidence of mild learning disability associated with each of the sex chromosome trisomies, although there is no evidence of intellectual disability in these persons.

Persons with karyotypes of 48,XXXY or 49,XXXXY have been reported but are extremely rare. These individuals show clinical outcomes similar to those seen in males with Klinefelter syndrome but with slightly increased severity. In these persons the "$n - 1$ rule" for X inactivation still holds, so that all but one of the X chromosomes present in each somatic cell is inactivated.

DISEASES ASSOCIATED WITH SINGLE-GENE MENDELIAN INHERITANCE

The term "Mendelian" is often used to denote patterns of genetic inheritance similar to those described

HUMAN GENETIC DISEASE

for traits in the garden pea by Gregor Mendel in the 1860s. Disorders associated with single-gene Mendelian inheritance are typically categorized as autosomal dominant, autosomal recessive, or sex-linked. Each category is described briefly in this section.

AUTOSOMAL DOMINANT INHERITANCE

A disease trait that is inherited in an autosomal dominant manner can occur in either sex and can be transmitted by either parent. It manifests itself in the heterozygote (designated Aa), who receives a mutant gene (designated a) from one parent and a normal ("wild-type") gene (designated A) from the other. In such a case the pedigree (i.e., a pictorial representation of family history) is vertical—that is, the disease passes from one generation to the next. The figure illustrates

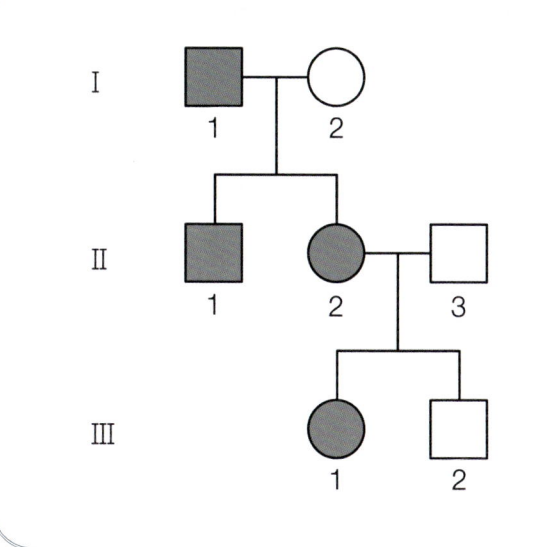

Pedigree of a family with a history of achondroplasia, an autosomal dominantly inherited disease. The solid symbols signify affected individuals.

the pedigree for a family with achondroplasia, an autosomal dominant disorder characterized by short-limbed dwarfism that results from a specific mutation in the fibroblast growth factor receptor 3 (*FGFR3*) gene. In pedigrees of this sort, circles refer to females and squares to males; two symbols directly joined at the midpoint represent a mating, and those suspended from a common overhead line represent siblings, with descending birth order from left to right. Solid symbols represent affected individuals, and open symbols represent unaffected individuals. The Roman numerals denote generations, whereas the Arabic numerals identify individuals within each generation. Each person listed in a pedigree may therefore be specified uniquely by a combination of one Roman and one Arabic numeral, such as II-1.

An individual who carries one copy of a dominant mutation (*Aa*) will produce two kinds of germ cells—eggs or sperm—typically in equal proportions; one half will bear the mutant gene (*A*), and the other will bear the normal gene (*a*). As a result, an affected heterozygote has a 50 percent chance of passing on the disease gene to each of his or her children. If an individual were to carry two copies of the dominant mutant gene (inherited from both parents), he or she would be homozygous (*AA*). The homozygote for a dominantly inherited abnormal gene may be equally affected with the heterozygote. Alternatively, he or she may be much more seriously affected; indeed, the homozygous condition may be lethal, sometimes even in utero or shortly after birth. Such is the case with achondroplasia, so that a couple with one affected partner and one unaffected partner will typically see half of their children affected, whereas a couple with both partners affected will see two-thirds of their surviving children affected and one-third unaffected, because 1 out of 4 conceptions will produce a homozygous fetus who will die before or shortly after birth.

Although autosomal dominant traits are typically evident in multiple generations of a family, they can also arise from new mutations, so that two unaffected parents, neither of whom carries the mutant gene in their somatic cells, can conceive an affected child. Indeed, for some disorders the new mutation rate is quite high; almost 7 out of 8 children with achondroplasia are born to two unaffected parents. Examples of autosomal dominant inheritance are common among human traits and diseases. More than 2,000 of these traits have been clearly identified.

In many genetic diseases, including those that are autosomal dominant, specific mutations associated with the same disease present in different families may be uniform, such that every affected individual carries exactly the same molecular defect (allelic homogeneity), or they may be heterogeneous, such that tens or even hundreds of different mutations, all affecting the same gene, may be seen in the affected population (allelic heterogeneity). In some cases even mutations in different genes can lead to the same clinical disorder (genetic heterogeneity). Achondroplasia is characterized by allelic homogeneity, such that essentially all affected individuals carry exactly the same mutation.

With regard to the physical manifestations (i.e., the phenotype) of some genetic disorders, a mutant gene may cause many different symptoms and may affect many different organ systems (pleiotropy). For example, along with the short-limbed dwarfism characteristic of achondroplasia, some individuals with this disorder also exhibit a long, narrow trunk, a large head with frontal bossing, and hyperextensibility of most joints, especially the knees. Similarly, for some genetic disorders, clinical severity may vary dramatically, even among affected members in the same family. These variations of phenotypic expression are called variable expressivity, and they are undoubtedly due to the modifying effects of other genes or environmental factors. Although for some disorders, such as achondroplasia, essentially all individuals carrying the mutant gene exhibit the disease phenotype, for other disorders some individuals who carry the mutant gene may express no apparent phenotypic abnormalities at all. Such unaffected individuals are called "nonpenetrant," although they can pass on the mutant gene to their offspring, who could be affected.

AUTOSOMAL RECESSIVE INHERITANCE

Nearly 2,000 traits have been related to single genes that are recessive; that is, their effects are masked by normal ("wild-type") dominant alleles and manifest themselves only in individuals homozygous for the mutant gene. For example, sickle cell anemia, a severe hemoglobin disorder, results only when a mutant gene (*a*) is inherited from both parents. Each of the latter is a carrier, a heterozygote with one normal gene and one mutant gene (*Aa*) who is phenotypically unaffected. The chance of such a couple producing a child with sickle cell anemia is one out of four for each pregnancy. For couples consisting of one carrier (*Aa*) and one affected individual (*aa*), the chance of their having an affected child is one out of two for each pregnancy.

Many autosomal recessive traits reflect mutations in key metabolic enzymes and result in a wide variety of disorders classified as inborn errors of metabolism. One of the best-known examples of this class of disorders is phenylketonuria (PKU), which results from mutations in the gene encoding the enzyme phenylalanine hydroxylase (PAH). PAH normally catalyzes the conversion of phenylalanine, an amino acid prevalent in dietary proteins and in the artificial

GENETIC TESTING AND GENE THERAPY

sweetener aspartame, to another amino acid called tyrosine. In persons with PKU, dietary phenylalanine either accumulates in the body or some of it is converted to phenylpyruvic acid, a substance that normally is produced only in small quantities. Individuals with PKU tend to excrete large quantities of this acid, along with phenylalanine, in their urine. When infants accumulate high concentrations of phenylpyruvic acid and unconverted phenylalanine

Pedigree of a family in which the gene for phenylketonuria is segregating. The half-solid circles and squares represent carriers of phenylketonuria; the solid symbols signify affected individuals.

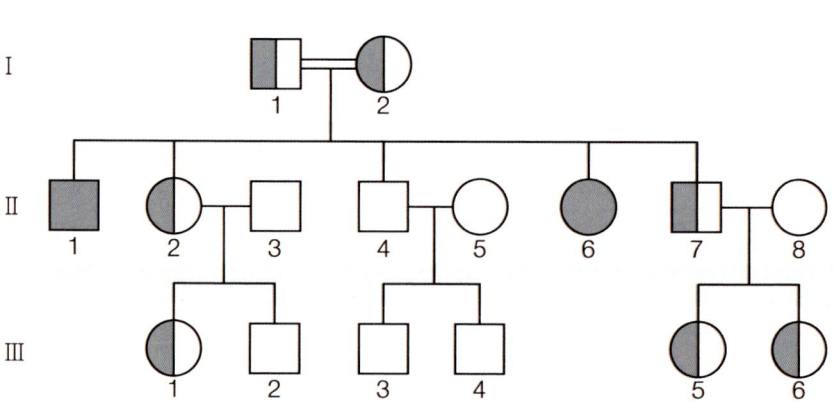

in their blood and other tissues, the consequence is intellectual disability. Fortunately, with early detection, strict dietary restriction of phenylalanine, and supplementation of tyrosine, intellectual disability can be prevented.

Since the recessive genes that cause inborn errors of metabolism are individually rare in the gene pool, it is not often that both parents are carriers; hence, the diseases are relatively uncommon. If the parents are related (consanguineous), however, they will be more likely to have inherited the same mutant gene from a common ancestor. For this reason, consanguinity is often more common in the parents of those with rare, recessive inherited diseases. The pedigree of a family in which PKU has occurred is shown in the figure. This pedigree demonstrates that the affected individuals for recessive diseases are usually siblings in one generation—the pedigree tends to be "horizontal," rather than "vertical" as in dominant inheritance.

SEX-LINKED INHERITANCE

In humans, there are hundreds of genes located on the X chromosome that have no counterpart on the Y chromosome. The traits governed by these genes thus show sex-linked inheritance. This type of inheritance has certain unique characteristics, which include the following: (1) There is no male-to-male (father-to-son) transmission, since sons will, by definition, inherit

GENETIC TESTING AND GENE THERAPY

the Y rather than the X chromosome. (2) The carrier female (heterozygote) has a 50 percent chance of passing the mutant gene to each of her children; sons who inherit the mutant gene will be hemizygotes and will manifest the trait, while daughters who receive the mutant gene will be unaffected carriers. (3) Males with the trait will pass the gene on to all of their daughters, who will be carriers. (4) Most sex-linked traits are recessively inherited, so that heterozygous females generally do not display the trait. The figure shows a pedigree of a family in which a mutant gene for hemophilia A, a sex-linked recessive disease, is

Pedigree of a family with a history of hemophilia A, a sex-linked recessively inherited disease. Half-solid circles represent female carriers (heterozygotes) of hemophilia A; the solid squares signify affected males (hemizygotes).

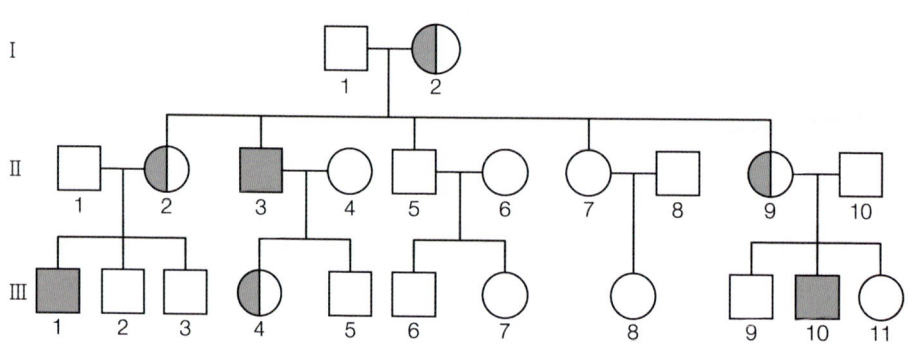

segregating. Hemophilia A gained notoriety in early studies of human genetics because it affected at least 10 males among the descendants of Queen Victoria, who was a carrier.

Hemophilia A, the most widespread form of hemophilia, results from a mutation in the gene encoding clotting factor VIII. Because of this mutation, affected males cannot produce functional factor VIII, so that their blood fails to clot properly, leading to significant and potentially life-threatening loss of blood after even minor injuries. Bleeding into joints commonly occurs as well and may be crippling. Therapy consists of avoiding trauma and of administering injections of purified factor VIII, which was once isolated from outdated human blood donations but can now be made in large amounts through recombinant DNA technology.

Although heterozygous female carriers of X-linked recessive mutations generally do not exhibit traits characteristic of the disorder, cases of mild or partial phenotypic expression in female carriers have been reported, resulting from nonrandom X inactivation.

DISEASES ASSOCIATED WITH SINGLE-GENE NON-MENDELIAN INHERITANCE

Although disorders resulting from single-gene defects that demonstrate Mendelian inheritance are perhaps better understood, it is now clear that a significant number of single-gene diseases also exhibit distinctly non-Mendelian patterns of inheritance. Among these are such disorders that result from triplet repeat expansions within or near specific genes (e.g., Huntington disease and fragile-X syndrome); a collection of neurodegenerative disorders, such as Leber hereditary optic neuropathy (LHON), that result from inherited mutations in the mitochondrial DNA; and diseases that result from mutations in imprinted genes (e.g., Angelman syndrome and Prader-Willi syndrome).

TRIPLET REPEAT EXPANSIONS

At least a dozen different disorders are now known to result from triplet repeat expansions in the human genome, and these fall into two groups: (1) those that involve a polyglutamine tract within the encoded protein product that becomes longer upon expansion of a triplet repeat, an example of which is Huntington disease, and (2) those that have unstable triplet repeats in noncoding portions of the gene that, upon expansion, interfere with appropriate expression of the gene product, an example of which is fragile-X syndrome.

HUMAN GENETIC DISEASE

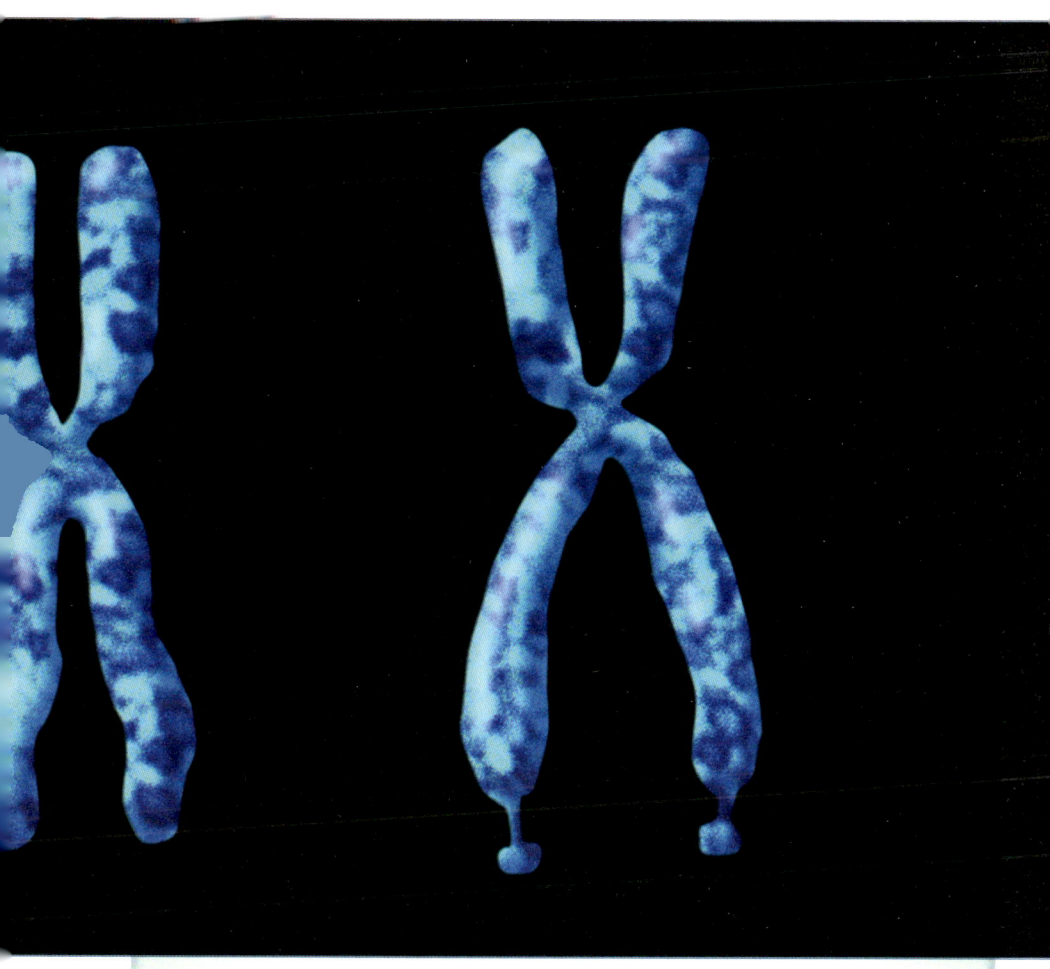

Compared to a normal X chromosome (left), a deformed chromosome associated with fragile-X syndrome (right) has a visibly abnormal site at the tip of the long arm.

Both groups of disorders exhibit a distinctive pattern of non-Mendelian inheritance termed anticipation, in which, following the initial appearance of the disorder in a given family, subsequent generations tend to show both increasing frequency and increasing severity of the disorder. This phenotypic anticipation is paralleled by increases in the relevant repeat length as it is passed from one generation to the next, with increasing size leading to increasing instability, until a "full expansion" mutation is achieved, generally several generations following the initial appearance of the disorder in the family. The full expansion mutation is then passed to subsequent generations in a standard Mendelian fashion—for example, autosomal dominant for Huntington disease and sex-linked for fragile-X syndrome.

MITOCHONDRIAL DNA MUTATIONS

Disorders resulting from mutations in the mitochondrial genome demonstrate an alternative form of non-Mendelian inheritance, termed "maternal inheritance," in which the mutation and disorder are passed from mothers—never from fathers—to all of their children. The mutations generally affect the function of the mitochondrion, compromising, among other processes, the production of cellular adenosine triphosphate (ATP). Severity and even penetrance can vary widely for disorders resulting from mutations in the mitochondrial DNA, generally believed to reflect the combined effects of heteroplasmy (i.e., mixed populations of both normal and mutant mitochondrial DNA in a single cell) and other confounding genetic or environmental factors. There are close to 50 mitochondrial genetic diseases currently known.

IMPRINTED GENE MUTATIONS

Some genetic disorders are now known to result from mutations in imprinted genes. Genetic imprinting involves a sex-specific process of chemical modification to the imprinted genes, so that they are expressed unequally, depending on the sex of the parent of origin. So-called maternally imprinted genes are generally expressed only when inherited from the father, and so-called paternally imprinted genes are generally expressed only when inherited from the mother. The disease gene associated with Prader-Willi syndrome is maternally imprinted, so that although every child inherits two copies of the gene (one maternal, one paternal), only the paternal copy is expressed. If the paternally inherited copy carries a mutation, the child will be left with no functional copies of the gene expressed, and the clinical traits of Prader-Willi syndrome will result. Similarly, the disease gene associated with Angelman syndrome is paternally imprinted, so that although every child inherits two copies of the gene, only the maternal copy is expressed. If the maternally inherited copy carries a mutation, the child again will be left with no functional copies of the gene expressed, and the clinical traits of Angelman syndrome will result. Individuals who carry the mutation but received it from the "wrong" parent can certainly pass it on to their children, although they will not exhibit clinical features of the disorder.

Upon rare occasion, persons are identified with an imprinted gene disorder who show no family history and do not appear to carry any mutation in the expected gene. These cases are now known to result from uniparental disomy, a phenomenon whereby a child is conceived who carries the normal complement of chromosomes but who has inherited both copies of a given chromosome from the same parent, rather than one from each parent, as is the normal fashion. If any key genes on that chromosome are imprinted in the parent of origin, the child may end up with no expressed copies, and a genetic disorder may result. Similarly, other genes may be overexpressed in cases of uniparental disomy, perhaps also leading to clinical complications. Finally, uniparental disomy can account for very rare instances whereby two parents, only one of whom is a carrier of an autosomal recessive mutation, can nonetheless have an affected child, in the circumstance that the child inherits two mutant copies from the carrier parent.

DISEASES CAUSED BY MULTIFACTORIAL INHERITANCE

Genetic disorders that are multifactorial in origin represent probably the single largest class of inherited disorders affecting the human population. By definition, these disorders involve the influence of multiple genes, generally acting in concert with environmental factors. Such common conditions as cancer, heart disease, and diabetes are now considered to be multifactorial disorders. Indeed, improvements in the tools used to study this class of disorders have enabled the assignment of specific contributing gene loci to a number of common traits and disorders. Identification and characterization of these contributing genetic factors may not only enable improved diagnostic and prognostic indicators but may also identify potential targets for future therapeutic intervention.

Because the genetic and environmental factors that underlie multifactorial disorders are often unknown, the risks of recurrence are usually arrived at empirically. In general, it can be said that risks of recurrence are not as great for multifactorial conditions as for single-gene diseases and that the risks vary with the number of relatives affected and the closeness of their relationship. Moreover, close relatives of more severely affected individuals (e.g., those with bilateral cleft lip and cleft palate) are generally at greater risk than those related to persons with a less-severe form of the same condition (e.g., unilateral cleft lip).

GENETICS OF CANCER

Although at least 90 percent of all cancers are sporadic, meaning that they do not seem to run in families, nearly 10 percent of cancers are now recognized as familial, and some are actually inherited in an apparently autosomal dominant manner. Cancer may therefore be considered a multifactorial disease, resulting from the combined influence of many genetic factors acting in concert with environmental insults (e.g., ultraviolet radiation, cigarette smoke, and viruses).

Cancers, both familial and sporadic, generally arise from alterations in one or more of three classes of genes: oncogenes, tumour suppressor genes, and genes whose products participate in genome surveillance—for example, in DNA damage repair. For familial cancers, affected members inherit one mutant copy of a gene that falls into one of the latter two classes. That mutation alone is not sufficient to cause cancer, but it predisposes individuals to the disease because they are now either more sensitive to spontaneous somatic mutations, as in the case of altered tumour suppressor genes, or are more prone to experience mutations, as in the case of impaired DNA repair enzymes. Of course, sporadic cancers can also arise from mutations in these same classes of genes, but because all of the mutations must arise in the individual *de novo*, as opposed to being inherited, they generally appear only later in life, and they do not run in families.

Retinoblastoma, an aggressive tumour of the eye that typically occurs in childhood, offers perhaps one of the clearest examples of the interplay between

HUMAN GENETIC DISEASE

inherited and somatic mutations in the genesis of cancer. Current data suggest that 60 to 70 percent of all cases of retinoblastoma are sporadic, while the rest are inherited. The relevant gene, RB, encodes a protein that normally functions as a suppressor of cell cycle progression and is considered a classic tumour suppressor gene. Children who inherit one mutant copy of the *RB* gene are at nearly 100 percent risk to develop retinoblastoma, because the probability that their one remaining functional *RB* gene will sustain a mutation in at least one retinal cell is nearly assured. In contrast, children who inherit two functional copies of the *RB* gene must experience two mutations at the *RB* locus in the same retinal cell in order to develop retinoblastoma; this is a very rare event. This "two-hit" hypothesis of retinoblastoma formation has provided a foundation upon which most subsequent theories of the genetic origins of familial cancer have been built.

Recent studies of both breast and colorectal cancers have revealed that, like retinoblastoma, these cancers are predominantly sporadic, although a small proportion are clearly familial. Sporadic breast cancer generally appears late in life, while the familial forms can present much earlier, often before age 40. For familial breast cancer, inherited mutations in one of two specific genes, *BRCA1* and *BRCA2*, account for at least half of the cases observed. The *BRCA1* and *BRCA2* genes both encode protein products believed to function in the pathways responsible for sensing and responding to DNA damage in cells. While a woman in the general population has about a 10 percent lifetime risk of developing breast cancer, half of all women with *BRCA1* or *BRCA2* mutations will develop breast cancer by age 50, and close to 90 percent will develop the disease by age 80. Women with *BRCA1* mutations are also at increased risk to develop ovarian tumours. As with retinoblastoma, both men and women who carry *BRCA1* or *BRCA2* mutations, whether they are personally affected or not, can pass the mutated gene to their offspring, although carrier daughters are much more likely than carrier sons to develop breast cancer.

Two forms of familial colorectal cancer, hereditary nonpolyposis colorectal cancer (HNPCC) and familial adenomatous polyposis (FAP), have also been linked to predisposing mutations in specific genes. Persons with familial HNPCC have inherited mutations in one or more of their DNA mismatch repair genes, predominantly *MSH2* or *MLH1*. Similarly, persons with FAP carry inherited mutations in their *APC* genes, the protein product of which normally functions as a tumour suppressor. For individuals in both categories, the combination of inherited and somatic mutations results in a nearly 100 percent lifetime risk of developing colorectal cancer.

Although most cancer cases are not familial, all are undoubtedly diseases of the genetic material of somatic cells. Studies of large numbers of both familial and sporadic cancers have led to the conclusion that cancer is a disease of successive mutations, acting in concert to deregulate normal cell growth, provide appropriate blood supply to the growing tumour, and ultimately enable tumour cell movement beyond normal tissue boundaries to achieve metastasis (i.e., the dissemination of cancer cells to other parts of the body).

Many of the agents that cause cancer (e.g., X-rays, certain chemicals) also cause mutations or chromosome abnormalities. For example, a large fraction of sporadic tumours have been found to carry oncogenes, altered forms of normal genes (proto-oncogenes) that have sustained a somatic "gain-of-function" mutation. An oncogene may be carried by a virus, or it can result from a chromosomal rearrangement, as is the case in chronic myelogenous leukemia, a cancer of the white blood cells characterized by the presence of the so-called Philadelphia chromosome in affected cells. The Philadelphia chromosome arises from a translocation in which one half of the long arm of chromosome 22 becomes attached to the end of the long arm of chromosome 9, creating the dominant oncogene *BCR/abl* at the junction point. The specific function of the *BCR/abl* fusion protein is not entirely clear. Another example is Burkitt lymphoma, in which a rearrangement between chromosomes places the *myc* gene from chromosome 8 under the influence of regulatory sequences that normally control expression of immunoglobulin genes. This deregulation of *myc*, a protein involved in mediating cell cycle progression, is thought to be one of the major steps in the formation of Burkitt lymphoma.

COGNITIVE AND BEHAVIORAL GENETICS

Mental activities, expressed in human behaviour, are intimately related to physical activities in the brain and nervous system. In 1929 British physician Sir Archibald Garrod emphasized this when he wrote: Each one of us differs from his fellows, not only in bodily structure and the proteins which enter into his composite, but apart from, or rather in consequence of, such individualities, men differ in mental outlook, character and ability.

Since that time, many investigators have sought to analyze the molecular and cellular components of behaviour in order to relate genes to such abstractions as intellect, temperament, and the emotions. Because the brain is ultimately responsible for behavioral development, neurobiologists have attempted to understand the unusual precision by which this organ's various regions are interconnected and the intricate chemical signals that, under genetic control, organize its complicated nerve fibre circuits.

Some of the most powerful experiments to dissect the "nature versus nurture" aspects of human intelligence and behaviour have involved studies of twins, both monozygotic (identical) and dizygotic (fraternal). Cognitive or behavioral characteristics that are entirely under genetic control would be predicted to be the same, or concordant, in monozygotic twins, who share identical genes regardless of their upbringing. These same characteristics would be predicted to be less concordant in dizygotic twins, who share, on average, only half of their genes.

Comparison of the concordance rates among monozygotic and dizygotic twins monitored for different traits allows an estimate of the heritability of those traits—that is, the proportion of population variation for a given trait that can be attributed to genes. A heritability value of 1.0 implies a purely genetic basis for a trait, and a value of 0.0 implies a purely environmental basis. Intelligence, measured as IQ, has a heritability value of 0.5, indicating that both genetics and environment play major roles in determining this trait. In contrast, schizophrenia has a value of 0.7, and both autism and bipolar disorder have heritability values of 1.0. Clearly, genetics play a large role in determining not only how our bodies look and function but also how we think and feel.

GENETIC DAMAGE FROM ENVIRONMENTAL AGENTS

We are exposed to many agents, both natural and man-made, that can cause genetic damage. Among these agents are viruses; compounds produced by plants, fungi, and bacteria; industrial chemicals; products of combustion; alcohol; ultraviolet and ionizing radiation; and even the oxygen that we breathe. Many of these agents have long been unavoidable, and consequently human beings have evolved defenses to minimize the damage that they cause and ways to repair the damage that cannot be avoided.

VIRUSES

Viruses survive by injecting their genetic material into living cells with the consequence that the biochemical machinery of the host cell is subverted from serving its own needs to serving the needs of the virus. During this process the viral genome often integrates itself into the genome of the host cell. This integration, or insertion, can occur either in the intergenic regions that make up the vast majority of human genomes, or it can occur in the middle of an important regulatory sequence or even in the region coding for a protein—i.e., a gene. In either of the latter two scenarios, the regulation or function of the interrupted gene is lost. If that gene encodes a protein that normally regulates cell division, the result may be unregulated cell growth and division. Alternatively, some viruses carry dominant oncogenes in their genomes, which can transform an infected cell and start it on the path toward cancer. Furthermore, viruses can cause mutations leading to cancer by the killing of the infected cell. Indeed, one of the body's defenses against viral infection involves recognizing and killing infected cells. The death of cells necessitates their replacement by the division of uninfected cells, and the more cell division that occurs, the greater the likelihood of a mutation arising from the small but finite infidelity in DNA replication. Among the viruses that can cause cancer are Epstein-Barr virus, papilloma viruses, hepatitis B and C viruses, retroviruses (e.g., human immunodeficiency virus), and herpes virus.

PLANTS, FUNGI, AND BACTERIA

During the ongoing struggle for survival, organisms have evolved toxic compounds as protection against predators or simply to gain competitive advantage. At the same time, these organisms have evolved mechanisms that make themselves immune to the effects of the toxins that they produce. Plants in particular utilize this strategy since they are rooted in place and cannot escape from predators. One-third of the dry weight of some plants can be accounted for by the toxic compounds that are collectively referred to as alkaloids. *Aspergillus flavus*, a fungus that grows on stored grain and peanuts, produces a powerful carcinogen called aflatoxin that can cause liver cancer. Bacteria produce many proteins that are toxic to the infected host, such as diphtheria toxin. They also produce proteins called bacteriocins that are toxic to other bacteria. Toxins can cause mutations indirectly by causing cell death, which necessitates replacement by cell division, thus enhancing the opportunity for mutation. Cyanobacteria that grow in illuminated surface water produce several carcinogens, such as microcystin, saxitoxin, and cylindrospermopsin, that can also cause liver cancer.

INDUSTRIAL CHEMICALS

Tens of thousands of different chemicals are routinely used in the production of plastics, fuels, food additives, and even medicines. Many of these chemicals are mutagens, and some have been found to be carcinogenic (cancer-producing) in rats or mice. A relatively easy and inexpensive test for mutagenicity, the Ames test, utilizes mutant strains of the bacterium *Salmonella typhimurium* and can be completed in a few days. Testing for carcinogenesis, on the other hand, is very time-consuming and expensive because the test substance must be administered to large numbers of laboratory animals, usually mice, for months before the tissues can be examined for cancers. For this reason, the number of known mutagens far exceeds the number of known carcinogens. Furthermore, animal tests for carcinogenesis are not completely predictive of the effects of the test chemical on humans for several reasons. First, the abilities of laboratory animals and humans to metabolize and excrete specific chemicals can differ greatly. In addition, in order to avoid the need to test each chemical at a range of doses, each chemical is usually administered at the maximum tolerated dose. At such high doses, toxicity and cell death occur, necessitating cell replacement by growth and cell division; cell division, in turn, increases the opportunity for mutation and hence for cancer. Alternatively, unusually high doses of a chemical may actually mask the carcinogenic potential of a compound because damaged cells may die rather than survive in mutated form.

COMBUSTION PRODUCTS

The burning of fossil fuels quite literally powers modern industrial societies. If the combustion of such fuels were complete, the products would be carbon dioxide and water. However, combustion is rarely complete, as is evidenced by the visible smoke issuing from chimneys and from the exhausts of diesel engines. Moreover, in addition to the particulates that we can see, incomplete combustion produces a witch's brew of volatile compounds that we do not see; and some of these, such as the dibenzodioxins, are intensely mutagenic and have been demonstrated to cause cancer in laboratory rodents. Epidemiological data indicate that dioxins are associated with increased risk of a

GENETIC TESTING AND GENE THERAPY

Cigarette smoking is a cause of cancer and many other health problems.

screening can identify only a limited number of common genetic conditions. Most genetic conditions are rare and difficult to detect.

If a diagnostic test reveals a positive result (i.e., that the fetus is affected by a genetic condition), the woman must decide whether to terminate the pregnancy or to continue with it and give birth to a disabled child. At that point it is essential that the woman receives unbiased and accurate information about the relevant condition and feels supported in making the right decision for her.

Most women who undergo screening or testing in pregnancy receive genetic counseling in some form, possibly from a midwife, general practice physician, or obstetrician rather than from an individual who specializes in genetic counseling. Such counseling may be cursory and directive, sometimes even eugenic. Both before and after testing, a woman should have access to the services of a trained genetic counselor to ensure that she can make genuinely informed decisions and be confident that she has made the right ones, as terminating a wanted pregnancy can be as distressing as giving birth to a child who will face lifelong physical or intellectual challenges.

INFANCY

Screening of large unphenotyped populations for evidence of genetic disease is currently pursued in

TESTING FOR GENETIC MUTATIONS

For parents wishing to avoid a genetic disorder in their child, a family history is not enough. Tests of the parents for possible genetic mutations are also not enough since a genetic disorder can occur in a child with parents who are not affected by the disorder. This situation arises when a gene mutation occurs in the egg or sperm (germinal mutation) or following conception, when chromosomes from the egg and sperm combine. Mutations can occur spontaneously or be stimulated by environmental factors, such as radiation or carcinogens (cancer-causing agents). Mutations occur with increasing frequency as people age. In men this may result from errors that occur throughout a lifetime as DNA (deoxyribonucleic acid) replicates to produce sperm. In women nondisjunction of chromosomes becomes more common later in life, increasing the risk of aneuploidy (too many or too few chromosomes). Because of this, it is not unusual for parents to seek prenatal genetic testing, although mutations can also occur after birth in either gender as a result of long-term exposure to ambient ionizing radiation. There also exist two broad classes of genes that are prone to mutations that give rise to cancer. These include oncogenes, which promote tumour growth, and tumour-suppressor genes, which suppress tumour growth.

most industrialized nations only in the newborn population, although future developments in the identification of risk genes for common adult onset disorders may change this policy. So-called mandated newborn screening was initiated in many societies in the latter quarter of the 20th century in an effort to prevent the drastic and often irreversible damage associated with a small number of relatively common genetic disorders whose sequelae can be either prevented or significantly relieved by early detection and intervention. The general practice is to collect a small sample of blood from each newborn within the first 72 hours of life, generally by pricking the infant's heel (or Guthrie test) and collecting drops of blood on special filter paper, which is then analyzed. Perhaps the best-known disorder screened in this manner is phenylketonuria (PKU), an autosomal recessive inborn error of metabolism. With early diagnosis and dietary intervention that is maintained throughout life, children with PKU can escape intellectual disability and grow into healthy adults who lead full and productive lives. Although many of the genetic disorders currently tested by mandated newborn screening are metabolic in nature, this trend is beginning to change. For example, in some communities newborns are screened for profound congenital hearing loss, which is now known to be frequently genetic in origin and for which effective intervention is now available (e.g., through cochlear implants).

Although hospitals seek parental consent prior to taking an infant's blood, no formal genetic counseling is provided unless it is requested or a positive result is found. Families with children who are directly affected by genetic conditions may seek genetic counseling. They may want to gain more information about particular conditions and why those conditions affect them, to explore the specific ways in which genetic conditions affect them, to seek advice about managing their child's condition, or to meet others who are similarly affected. Many genetic counselors specialize in certain groups of genetic conditions, such as bone dysplasias and metabolic conditions. Such counselors tend to be familiar with the day-to-day effects of living with particular genetic conditions and can help individuals to find appropriate support groups.

ADULTHOOD

At present, adults are generally tested for evidence of genetic disease only if personal or family history suggests they are at increased risk for a given disorder. A typical example would be a young man whose father, paternal aunt, and older brother have all been diagnosed with early onset colorectal cancer. Although this person may appear perfectly healthy, he is at significantly increased risk to carry mutations associated with familial colorectal cancer, and accurate genetic testing could enable heightened surveillance (e.g., frequent colonoscopies) that might ultimately save his life.

Carrier testing for adults in most developed nations is generally offered only if family history or ethnic origins suggest an increased risk of having a particular disease. A typical example would be to offer carrier testing for cystic fibrosis to a couple including one member who has a sibling with the disorder. Another would be to offer carrier testing for Tay-Sachs disease to couples of Ashkenazic Jewish origin, a population known to carry an increased frequency of Tay-Sachs mutations. The same would be true for couples of African or Mediterranean descent with regard to sickle cell anemia or thalassemia, respectively. Typically, in each of these cases a genetic counselor would be involved to help the individuals or couples understand their options and make informed decisions.

In general, genetic testing in adulthood has become increasingly oriented toward predictive testing, which is aimed at determining whether a person is at

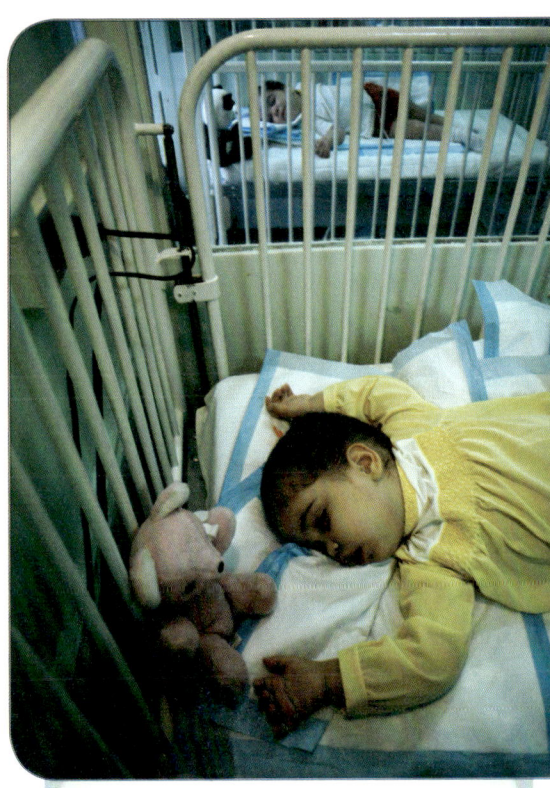

This baby has Tay-Sachs, a disease that occurs most commonly among Ashkenazi Jews.

risk of developing a late-onset genetic condition (e.g., Huntington disease and some forms of cancer) or has a genetic predisposition to a common disease (e.g., heart disease). Before individuals begin the predictive testing process, genetic counseling is advisable. Discovering that one is going to develop an incurable late-onset disease can be traumatic. Individuals in affected families may not wish to know their status if there is nothing they can do to avoid their fate. Even when preventive action is possible—for example, mastectomy to minimize the risk of breast cancer—that knowledge itself can be traumatic. Also, some recommended preventive actions may be hard for individuals to comply with (e.g., behavioral or dietary changes). There is evidence that many individuals have difficulty understanding risk percentages. Without the benefit of counseling, some may underestimate their risk. Alternatively, some individuals who receive diagnoses of genetic conditions may believe that they are facing an unavoidable fate even though preventive action may be effective.

TYPES OF DIAGNOSTIC GENETIC TESTS

Once the decision is made to pursue a diagnosis, genetic testing in undertaken. Chemical, radiological, histopathologic, and electrodiagnostic procedures can diagnose basic defects in patients suspected of genetic disease. Genetic tests may involve cytogenetic analyses to investigate chromosomes, molecular assays to investigate genes and DNA, or biochemical assays to investigate enzymes, hormones, or amino acids. Tests such as amino acid chromatography of blood and urine, in which the amino acids present in these fluids are separated on the basis of certain chemical affinities, can be used to identify specific hereditary or acquired gene defects. There also exist numerous genetic tests for blood and blood typing and antibody determination. These tests are used to isolate blood or antibody abnormalities that can be traced to genes involved in the generation of these substances. Various electrodiagnostic procedures such as electromyography are useful for identifying defects in muscle and nerve function, which often result from inherited gene mutations.

TESTING FOR PRENATAL DIAGNOSIS

Perhaps one of the most sensitive areas of medical genetics is prenatal diagnosis, the genetic testing of an unborn fetus, because of fears of eugenic misuse or because some couples may choose to terminate a pregnancy depending on the outcome of the test. Nonetheless, prenatal testing in one form or another is now almost ubiquitous in most industrialized nations, and recent advances both in testing technologies and in the set of "risk factor" genes to be screened promise to make prenatal diagnosis even more widespread. Indeed, parents may soon be able to ascertain information not only about the sex and health status of their unborn child but also about his or her complexion, personality, and intellect. Whether parents should have access to all of this information and how they may choose to use it are matters of much debate.

Current forms of prenatal diagnosis can be divided into two classes, those that are apparently noninvasive and those that are more invasive. At present the noninvasive tests are generally offered to all pregnant women, while the more-invasive tests are generally recommended only if some risk factors exist. The noninvasive tests include ultrasound imaging and maternal serum tests. Serum tests include one for alphafetoprotein (AFP) or one for alphafetoprotein, estriol, and human chorionic gonadotropin (triple screen). These tests serve as screens for structural fetal malformations and for neural tube closure defects. The triple screen also can detect some cases of Down syndrome, although there is a significant false-positive and false-negative rate.

The AFP test involves screening for alphafetoprotein (AFP) in maternal serum. Elevated levels of AFP are associated with neural tube defects in the fetus, including spina bifida (defective closure of the spine) and anencephaly (absence of brain tissue). When AFP levels are elevated, a more specific diagnosis is attempted, using ultrasound and amniocentesis to analyze the amniotic fluid for

GENETIC COUNSELING AND TESTING

the presence of AFP. Fetal cells contained in the amniotic fluid also can be cultured and the karyotype (chromosome morphology) determined to identify chromosomal abnormality. Cells for chromosome analysis also can be obtained by chorionic villus sampling, the direct needle aspiration of cells from the chorionic villus (future placenta).

More-invasive tests include amniocentesis, chorionic villus sampling, percutaneous umbilical blood sampling, and, upon rare occasion, preimplantation testing of either a polar body or a dissected embryonic cell. Amniocentesis is a procedure in which a long, thin needle is inserted through the abdomen and uterus into the amniotic sac, enabling the removal of a small amount of the amniotic fluid bathing the fetus. This procedure is generally performed under ultrasound guidance between the 15th and 17th weeks of pregnancy, and, although it is generally regarded as safe, complications can occur, ranging from cramping to infection or loss of the fetus. The amniotic fluid obtained can be used in each of three ways: (1) living fetal cells recovered from this fluid can be induced to grow and can be analyzed to assess chromosome number, composition, or structure; (2) cells recovered from the fluid can be used for molecular studies; and (3) the amniotic fluid itself can be analyzed biochemically to determine the relative abundance of a variety of compounds associated with normal or abnormal fetal metabolism and development. Amniocentesis is typically offered to pregnant women over age 35, because of the significantly increased rate of chromosome disorders observed in the children of older mothers. A clear advantage of amniocentesis is the wealth of material obtained and the relative safety of the procedure. The disadvantage is timing: results may not be received until the pregnancy is already into the 19th week or beyond, at which point the possibility of termination may be much more physically and emotionally wrenching than if considered earlier.

Chorionic villus sampling (CVS) is a procedure in which either a needle is inserted through the abdomen or a thin tube is inserted into the vagina and cervix to obtain a small sample of placental tissue called chorionic villi. CVS has the advantage of being performed earlier in the pregnancy (generally 10–11 weeks), although the risk of complications is greater than that for amniocentesis. Risks associated with CVS include fetal loss and fetal limb reduction if the procedure is performed earlier than 10 weeks gestation. Another disadvantage of CVS reflects the tissue sampled: chorionic villi are not part of the embryo, and such a sample may not accurately represent the embryonic genetic constitution. In contrast, amniotic cells are embryonic in origin, having been sloughed off into the fluid. Therefore, abnormalities, often chromosomal, may be seen in the chorionic villi but not in the fetus, or vice versa.

GENETIC COUNSELING AND TESTING

Women who have had repeated in vitro fertilization failures may undergo preimplantation genetic diagnosis (PGD). PGD is used to detect the presence of embryonic genetic abnormalities that have a high likelihood of causing implantation failure or miscarriage. In PGD a single cell is extracted from the embryo and is analyzed by fluorescence in situ hybridization (FISH), a technique used to identify structural abnormalities in chromosomes that standard tests such as karyotyping cannot detect. In some cases DNA is isolated from the cell and analyzed by polymerase chain reaction (PCR) for the detection of

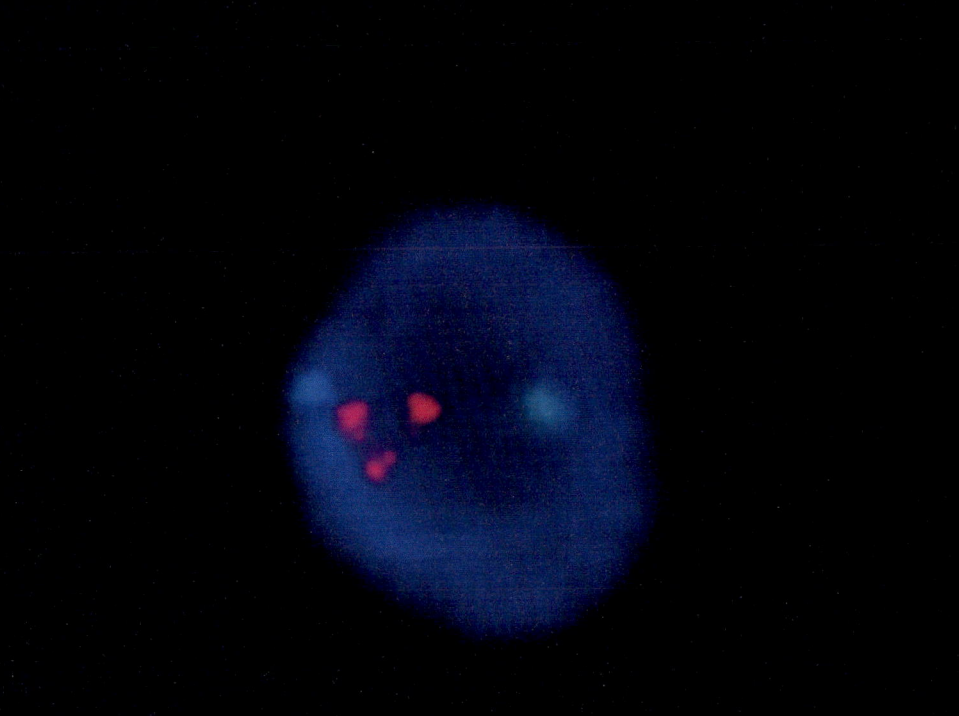

The nucleus of this cell, analyzed by fluorescence in situ hybridization, reveals three copies of chromosome 21, indicating Down syndrome.

gene mutations that can give rise to certain disorders such as Tay-Sachs disease.

Another technique, known as comparative genomic hybridization (CGH), may be used alongside PGD to identify chromosomal abnormalities. Both percutaneous umbilical blood sampling (PUBS) and preimplantation testing are rare, relatively high-risk, and performed only in very unusual cases. Preimplantation testing of embryos derived by in vitro fertilization is a particularly new technique and is currently used only in cases of couples who are at high risk for having a fetus affected with a given familial genetic disorder and who find all other alternatives unacceptable. Preimplantation testing involves obtaining eggs and sperm from the couple, combining them in the laboratory, and allowing the resultant embryos to grow until they reach the early blastocyst stage of development, at which point a single cell is removed from the rest and harvested for fluorescent in situ hybridization (FISH) or molecular analysis. The problem with this procedure is that one cell is scant material for diagnosis, so that a large array of tests cannot be performed. Similarly, if the test fails for any technical reason, it cannot be repeated. Finally, embryos determined to be normal and therefore selected for implantation into the mother are subject to other complications normally associated with in vitro fertilization—namely, that only a small fraction of the implanted embryos make it to term and that multiple, and therefore high-risk, pregnancies are common. Nonetheless, many at-risk couples find these complications easier to accept than the elective termination of the pregnancy.

It should be noted that researchers have identified fetal cells in the maternal circulation and that procedures are currently under development to enable their isolation and analysis, thereby providing a noninvasive alternative for molecular prenatal testing. Although these techniques are currently experimental and are not yet available for clinical application, they may well become the methods of choice in the future.

Advances in DNA sequencing technologies have enabled scientists to reconstruct the human fetal genome from genetic material found in maternal blood and paternal saliva. This in turn has raised the possibility for development of prenatal diagnostic tests that are noninvasive to the fetus but capable of accurately detecting genetic defects in fetal DNA. Such tests are desirable because they would significantly reduce the risk of miscarriage that is associated with procedures requiring cell sampling from the fetus or chorionic villus.

KARYOTYPING

Chromosomal karyotyping, in which chromosomes are arranged according to a standard classification

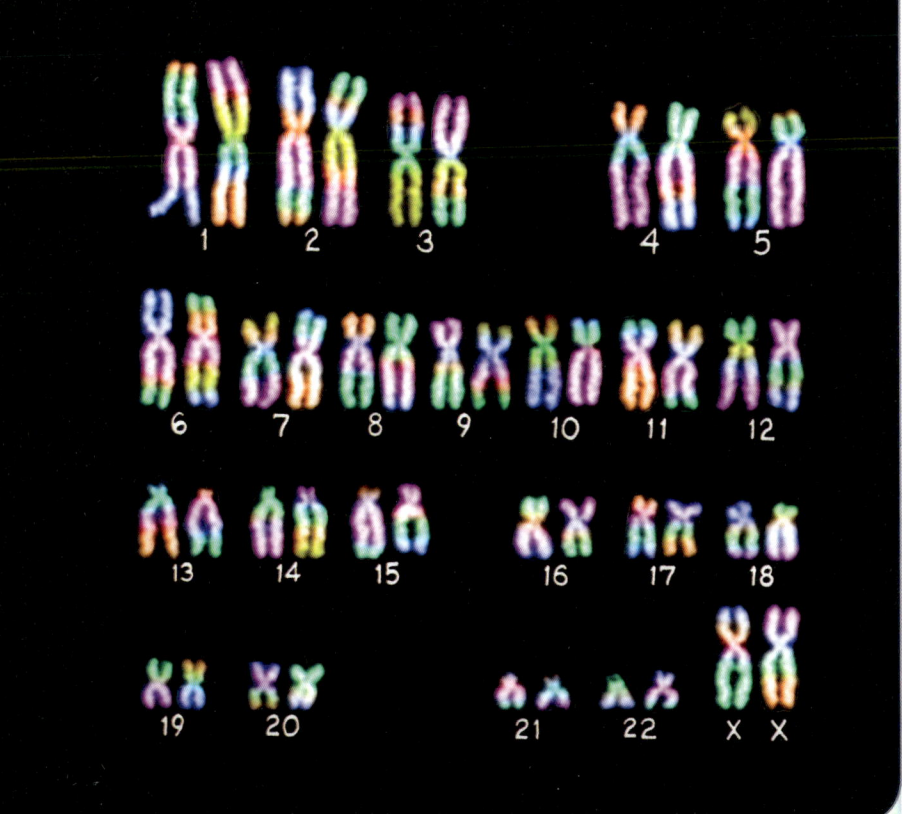

A colour-enhanced karyotype of a normal human female, showing 22 pairs of autosomes and two X chromosomes.

scheme, is one of the most commonly used genetic tests. To obtain a person's karyotype, laboratory technicians grow human cells in tissue culture media. After being stained and sorted, the chromosomes are counted and displayed. The cells are obtained from the blood, skin, or bone marrow or by amniocentesis or chorionic villus sampling, as noted above. The standard karyotype has approximately 400 visible bands, and each band contains up to several hundred genes.

GENETIC COUNSELING AND TESTING

When a chromosomal aberration is identified, it allows for a more accurate prediction of the risk of its recurrence in future offspring. Karyotyping can be used not only to diagnose aneuploidy, which is responsible for Down syndrome, Turner syndrome, and Klinefelter syndrome, but also to identify the chromosomal aberrations associated with solid tumours such as nephroblastoma, meningioma, neuroblastoma, retinoblastoma, renal-cell carcinoma, small-cell lung cancer, and certain leukemias and lymphomas.

Karyotyping requires a great deal of time and effort and may not always provide conclusive information. It is most useful in identifying very large defects involving hundreds or even thousands of genes.

DNA TESTS

Techniques such as FISH, CGH, and PCR have high rates of sensitivity and specificity. These procedures provide results more quickly than traditional karyotyping because no cell culture is required. FISH can detect genetic deletions involving one to five genes. It is also useful in detecting moderate-sized deletions, such as those causing Prader-Willi syndrome. CGH is more sensitive than FISH and is capable of detecting a variety of small chromosomal rearrangements, deletions, and duplications. The analysis of individual genes also has been greatly enhanced by the development of PCR and recombinant DNA technology. In

GENETIC TESTING AND GENE THERAPY

recombinant DNA technology, small DNA fragments are isolated and copied, thereby producing unlimited amounts of cloned material. Once cloned, the various genes and gene products can be used to study gene function both in healthy individuals and those with disease. Recombinant DNA and PCR methods can detect any change in DNA, down to a one-base-pair change, such as a point mutation or a single nucleotide polymorphism, out of the three billion base pairs in the human genome. The detection of these

The process of DNA extraction is necessary to isolate molecules of DNA from cells or tissues. A series of steps, including the use of protease enzymes to strip proteins from the DNA, is required for isolating pure DNA that is suitable for use in later procedures, such as cloning or sequencing.

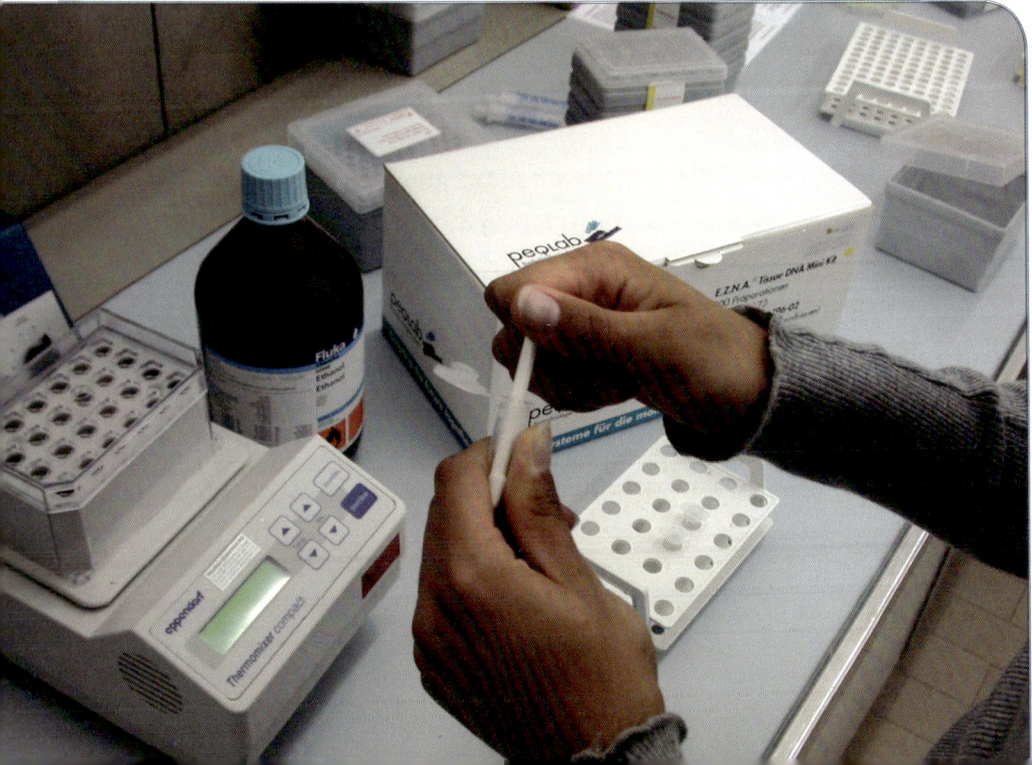

GENETIC TESTING AND GENEALOGY

Genealogy in the modern era has become grounded in the science of genetics. Increased rigour in the field has been made possible by the development and ongoing refinement of methods to accurately trace genes and genetic variations through generations. In some instances, in the process of tracing genetic lineages, gene variations associated with disease may be detected.

Methods used in genealogical genetics analysis include Y chromosome testing, mitochondrial DNA (mtDNA) testing, and detection of ancestry-associated genetic variants that occur as single nucleotide polymorphisms (SNPs) in the human genome. Y chromosome testing is based on genetic comparison of Y chromosomes, from males. Such analyses allow genealogists to confirm whether males with the same surname are related. Likewise, maternal lineages can be traced genetically through mtDNA testing, since the mitochondrial genome is inherited only from the mother.

Following the completion of the Human Genome Project in 2003, it became possible to more efficiently scan the human genome for SNPs and to compare SNPs occurring in the genomes of human populations in different geographical regions of the world. In 2010 a study using genome-wide SNP analysis incorporating ancestral information successfully traced persons in Europe to the villages in which their grandparents lived.

changes is facilitated by DNA probes that are labeled with radioactive isotopes or fluorescent dyes. Such methods can be used to identify persons who are carriers for inherited conditions, such as hemophilia A, polycystic kidney disease, sickle cell anemia, Huntington disease, cystic fibrosis, and hemochromatosis.

BIOCHEMICAL TESTS

Biochemical tests primarily detect enzymatic defects such as phenylketonuria, porphyria, and glycogen-storage disease. Although testing of newborns for all these abnormalities is possible, it is not cost-effective, because some of these conditions are quite rare. Screening requirements for these disorders vary and depend on whether the disease is sufficiently common, has severe consequences, and can be treated or prevented if diagnosed early and whether the test can be applied to the entire population at risk.

TESTING FOR DIAGNOSIS AFTER THE NEONATAL PERIOD

In the case of genetic disease, options often exist for presymptomatic diagnosis—that is, diagnosis of individuals at risk for developing a given disorder, even though at the time of diagnosis they may be clinically healthy. Options may even exist for carrier testing, studies that determine whether an individual is at increased risk of having a child with a given disorder, even though he or she personally may never display symptoms. Accurate predictive information can enable early intervention, which often prevents the clinical onset of symptoms and the irreversible damage that may have already occurred by waiting for symptoms and then responding to them. In the case of carrier testing, accurate information can enable prospective parents to make more-informed family-planning decisions. Unfortunately, there can also be negative aspects to early detection, including such issues as privacy, individual responses to potentially negative information, discrimination in the workplace, or discrimination in access to or cost of health or life insurance. While some governments have outlawed the use of presymptomatic genetic testing information by insurance companies and employers, others have embraced it as a way to bring spiraling health-care costs under control. Some communities have even considered instituting premarital carrier testing for common disorders in the populace.

The use of genetic testing procedures for diagnosis of a genetic disorder after the prenatal and neonatal periods can be divided into two different groups as previously mentioned: (1) testing of individuals considered at risk from phenotype or family history and (2) screening of entire populations, regardless of phenotype or personal family history, for evidence of genetic disorders common in that population. Both forms are currently pursued in many societies. Indeed, with the explosion of information about the human genome and the increasing identification of potential "risk genes" for common disorders, such as cancer, heart disease, or diabetes, the role of predictive genetic screening in general medical practice is likely to increase.

Genetic tests themselves can take many forms, and the choice of tests depends on a number of factors. For example, screening for evidence of sickle cell anemia, a hemoglobin disorder, is generally pursued at least initially by tests involving the hemoglobin proteins themselves, rather than DNA, because the relevant gene product (blood) is readily accessible, and because the protein test is currently cheaper to perform than the DNA test. In contrast, screening for cystic fibrosis, a disorder that predominantly affects the lungs and pancreas, is generally pursued in the at-risk newborn at the level of DNA because there is no cheap and accurate alternative. Older persons suspected of having cystic fibrosis, however, can also be diagnosed with a "sweat test" that measures sweat electrolytes.

Tests involving analysis of DNA are particularly powerful because they can be performed using very tiny samples; also, the DNA tested can originate from almost any tissue type, regardless of whether the gene of interest happens to be expressed in that tissue.

GENETIC COUNSELING AND TESTING

Current technologies applied for mutation detection include traditional karyotyping and Southern blotting, as well as a multitude of new tests, including FISH with specific probes or the polymerase chain reaction (PCR), which refers to an enzymatic process by which specific regions of the genome can be amplified for molecular study. Which tests are applied depends on whether the genetic abnormalities are likely to be chromosomal (in which case karyotyping or FISH are appropriate), large deletions or other rearrangements (best tested for by Southern blotting or PCR), or point mutations (best confirmed by PCR followed by oligonucleotide hybridization or restriction enzyme digestion). If a large number of different point mutations are sought, as is often the case, the most appropriate technology may be microarray hybridization analysis, which can test for tens to hundreds of thousands of different point mutations in the same sample simultaneously.

Advances made in genetic diagnostic testing have led to meaningful diagnosis of a variety of genetic disorders and diseases. Testing is done in conjunction with genetic counseling, not because the recipients of a diagnosis must take a specific action, but because there are many things to consider when deciding what course of action to take in light of the diagnosis.

CHAPTER 4
GENE THERAPY

Gene therapy, also called gene transfer therapy, is the introduction of a normal gene into an individual's genome in order to repair a mutation that causes a genetic disease. The promise of gene therapy lies in the fact that when a normal gene is inserted into the nucleus of a mutant cell, the gene most likely will integrate into a chromosomal site different from the defective allele. Although that may repair the mutation, a new mutation may result if the normal gene integrates into another functional gene. If the normal gene replaces the mutant allele, there is a chance that the transformed cells will proliferate and produce enough normal gene product for the entire body to be restored to the undiseased phenotype. Traditionally, the gene has been inserted into a cell. With advances in stem cell technology, it may be possible to use induced pluripotent stem cells (iPSCs) to introduce disease-free cells that are an exact match for the individual.

MAPPING THE HUMAN GENOME

A map of the human genome was an essential first step to gene therapy. The Human Genome Project (HGP) was launched in 1990 in the United States for that purpose. An early aim of the HGP was to obtain the whole genome sequences of important experimental model organisms such as the fruit fly *Drosophila melanogaster*. In sequencing smaller and therefore more-tractable genomes, three outcomes were anticipated. First, the sequences would be of value to the research community, serving to accelerate efforts to understand gene function by using model systems. Second, the experience gained would inform approaches to sequencing the human genome and other similarly sized genomes. Third, functional relationships between sequences of different organisms would be revealed as a consequence of cross-species sequence similarity. With the involvement of more than one thousand scientists worldwide, two human genome sequences were published in 2001. Methods and analytic standards were established for use in sequencing other large genomes. An important approach involved hierarchical shotgun sequencing, in which segments of genomic DNA were cloned

Bands of DNA representing a segment of the human genome.

(copied) and arranged into ordered arrays. Those ordered arrays, known as physical maps, served to break large genomes into thousands of short DNA fragments. Those short fragments were then aligned with identical sequences overlapped, enabling the fragments to be linked together to yield the full-length genomic sequence.

With an understanding and "map" of the human genome, scientists were finally able to examine a person's DNA and identify the cause of a genetic disease. With this knowledge, they could set about correcting the defect through gene therapy or—as we gain more expertise—to use induced pluripotent stem cells (iPSCs) in conjunction with gene therapy. (To use traditional cell therapy, in which a patient is treated with his own cells would not be workable because those cells would contain the corrupted genetic code.)

PREREQUISITES FOR GENE THERAPY

Prerequisites for gene therapy include finding the best delivery system (often a virus, typically referred to as a viral vector) for the gene, demonstrating that the transferred gene can express itself in the host cell, and establishing that the procedure is safe. Few clinical trials of gene therapy in humans have satisfied all those conditions, often because the delivery system fails to reach cells or the genes are not expressed by

REGULATION OF GENE THERAPY CLINICAL TRIALS

A clinical trial involves the use of human participants in research for the purpose of adding to medical knowledge. The participants in a clinical trial are not forced to participate. They volunteer for the opportunity because often the treatments they will receive are only available to them through this mechanism. Often these volunteers do not have other treatment options to pursue. They must sign an informed consent document as proof that they are aware of any possible adverse consequences.

Clinical trails are highly regulated. There is a protocol, or plan, for the study. Rigorous criteria are in place for the selection of volunteers. In some clinical trials, whether the volunteer is receiving the treatment or serving as a control is not known to the participant or the people administering the treatments. Trials are overseen by medical professionals, and the participants are free to withdraw from the trial at any time.

Every federally supported or conducted trial of a drug, biological product, or medical device that is regulated by the FDA must be overseen by an institutional review board (IRB). The IRB reviews, approves, and monitors the study. Clinical trials involving gene therapy are subject to rigorous review because genetic material is involved in these protocols.

cells. Improved gene therapy systems are being developed by using nanotechnology. A promising application of that research involves packaging genes into nanoparticles that are targeted to cancer cells, thereby killing cancer cells and leaving healthy cells unharmed.

NANOTECHNOLOGY RESEARCH

Nanotechnology promises to impact medical treatment in multiple ways. First, advances in nanoscale particle design and fabrication provide new options for drug delivery and drug therapies. More than half of the new drugs developed each year are not water-soluble, which makes their delivery difficult. In the form of nanosized particles, however, these drugs are more readily transported to their destination, and they can be delivered in the conventional form of pills.

More important, nanotechnology may enable drugs to be delivered to precisely the right location in the body and to release drug doses on a predetermined schedule for optimal treatment. The general approach is to attach the drug to a nanosized carrier that will release the medicine in the body over an extended period of time or when specifically triggered to do so. In addition, the surfaces of these nanoscale carriers may be treated to seek out and become localized at a disease site—for example, attaching to

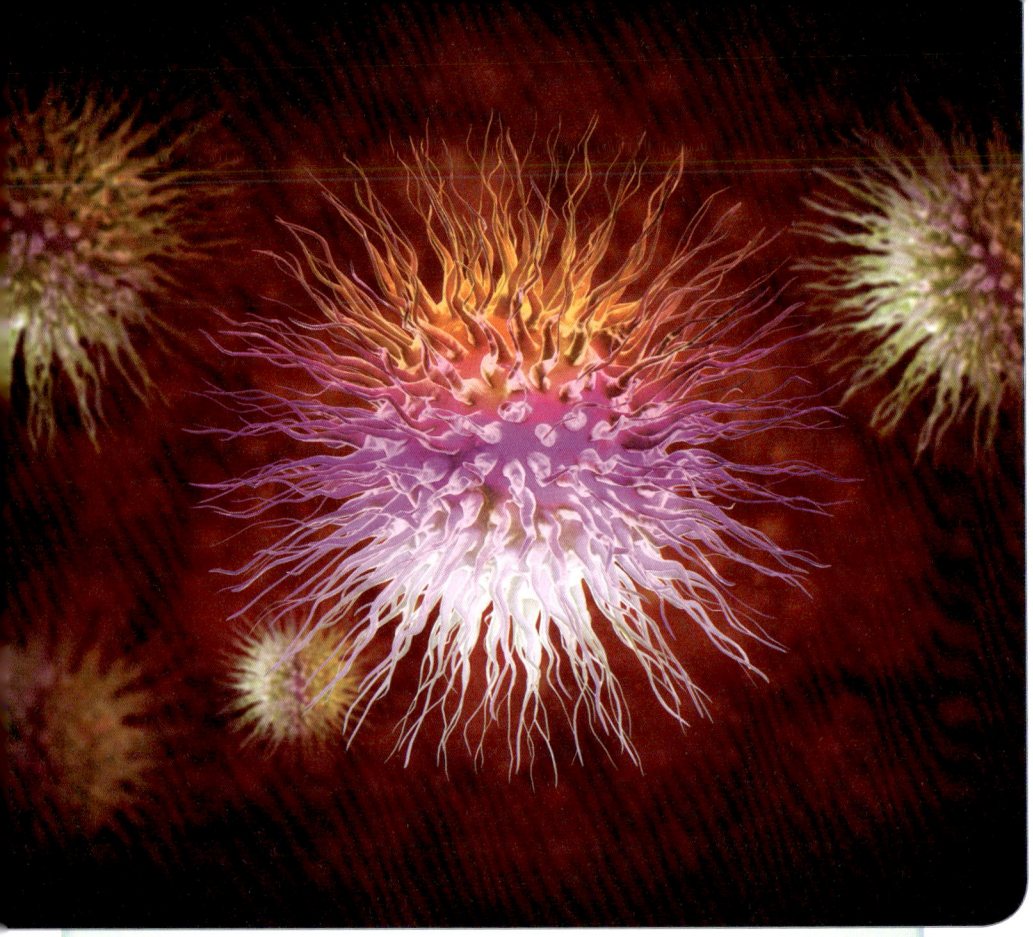

Synthetic dendrimers are being used in nanotechnology.

cancerous tumours. One type of molecule of special interest for these applications is an organic dendrimer. A dendrimer is a special class of polymeric molecule that weaves in and out from a hollow central region. These spherical "fuzz balls" are about the size of a typical protein but cannot unfold like proteins. Interest in dendrimers derives from the ability to tailor their cavity sizes and chemical properties to hold different therapeutic agents. Researchers hope to design different dendrimers that can swell and release their drug on exposure to specifically recognized molecules that indicate a disease target. This same general approach to nanoparticle-directed drug delivery is being explored for other types of nanoparticles as well.

Another approach involves gold-coated nanoshells whose size can be adjusted to absorb light energy at different wavelengths. In particular, infrared light will pass through several centimetres of body tissue, allowing a delicate and precise heating of such capsules in order to release the therapeutic substance within. Furthermore, antibodies may be attached to the outer gold surface of the shells to cause them to bind specifically to certain tumour cells, thereby reducing the damage to surrounding healthy cells.

A second area of intense study in nanomedicine is that of developing new diagnostic tools. Motivation for this work ranges from fundamental biomedical research at the level of single genes or cells to point-of-care applications for health delivery services. With advances in molecular biology, much diagnostic work now focuses on detecting specific biological "signatures." These analyses are referred to as bioassays. Examples include studies to determine which genes are active in response to a particular disease or drug therapy. A general approach involves attaching fluorescing dye molecules to the target biomolecules in order to reveal their concentration.

Another approach to bioassays uses semiconductor nanoparticles, such as cadmium selenide, which emit light of a specific wavelength depending on their size. Different-size particles can be tagged to different receptors so that a wider variety of distinct colour tags are available than can be distinguished for dye molecules. The degradation in fluorescence with repeated excitation for dyes is avoided. Furthermore, various-size particles can be encapsulated in latex beads and their resulting wavelengths read like a bar code. This approach, while still in the exploratory stage, would allow for an enormous number of distinct labels for bioassays.

Another nanotechnology variation on bioassays is to attach one half of the single-stranded complementary DNA segment for the genetic sequence to be detected to one set of gold particles and the other half to a second set of gold particles. When the material of interest is present in a solution, the two attachments cause the gold balls to agglomerate, providing a large change in optical properties that can be seen in the colour of the solution. If both halves of the sequence do not match, no agglomeration will occur and no change will be observed.

Approaches that do not involve optical detection techniques are also being explored with nanoparticles. For example, magnetic nanoparticles can be attached to antibodies that in turn recognize and attach to specific biomolecules. The magnetic particles then act as tags and "handlebars" through which magnetic fields can be used for mixing, extracting, or identifying the attached biomolecules within microlitre- or nanolitre-sized samples. For example, magnetic nanoparticles stay magnetized as a single domain for a significant period, which enables them to be aligned and detected in a magnetic field. In particular, attached antibody–magnetic-nanoparticle combinations rotate slowly and give a distinctive magnetic signal. In contrast, magnetically tagged antibodies that are not attached to the biological material being detected rotate more rapidly and so do not give the same distinctive signal.

Microfluidic systems, or "labs-on-chips," have been developed for biochemical assays of minuscule samples. Typically cramming numerous electronic and mechanical components into a portable unit no larger than a credit card, they are especially useful for conducting rapid analysis in the field. While these microfluidic systems primarily operate at the microscale (that is, millionths of a metre), nanotechnology has contributed new concepts and will likely play an increasing role in the future. For example, separation of DNA is sensitive to entropic effects, such as the entropy required to unfold DNA of a given length. A new approach to separating DNA could take advantage of its passage through a nanoscale array of posts or channels such that DNA molecules of different lengths would uncoil at different rates.

Other researchers have focused on detecting signal changes as nanometre-wide DNA strands are threaded through a nanoscale pore. Early studies used pores punched in membranes by viruses; artificially fabricated nanopores are also being tested. By applying an electric potential across the membrane in a liquid cell to pull the DNA through, changes in ion current can be measured as different repeating base units of the molecule pass through the pores. Nanotechnology-enabled advances in the entire area of bioassays will clearly impact health care in many ways, from early detection, rapid clinical analysis, and home monitoring to new understanding of molecular biology and genetic-based treatments for fighting disease.

RECOMBINANT DNA TECHNOLOGY

Recombinant DNA technology joins DNA molecules from two different species and inserts the material into a host organism to produce new genetic combinations that are of value to science, medicine, agriculture, and industry. Since the focus of all genetics is the gene, the fundamental goal of laboratory geneticists is to isolate, characterize, and manipulate genes. Although it is relatively easy to isolate a sample of DNA from a collection of cells, finding a specific gene within this DNA sample can be compared to finding a needle in a haystack. Consider the fact that each human cell contains approximately 2 metres (6 feet) of DNA. Therefore, a small tissue sample will contain many kilometres of DNA. However, recombinant DNA technology has made it possible to isolate one gene or any other segment of DNA, enabling researchers to determine its nucleotide sequence, study its transcripts, mutate it in highly specific ways, and reinsert the modified sequence into a living organism.

DNA CLONING

In biology a clone is a group of individual cells or organisms descended from one progenitor. This means that the members of a clone are genetically identical, because cell replication produces identical daughter cells each time. The use of the word "clone" has been extended to recombinant DNA technology, which has provided scientists with the ability to produce many copies of a single fragment of DNA, such as a gene, creating identical copies that constitute a DNA clone. In practice the procedure is carried out by inserting a DNA fragment into a small DNA molecule and then allowing this molecule to replicate inside a simple living cell such as a bacterium. The small replicating molecule is called a DNA vector (carrier). The most commonly used vectors are plasmids (circular DNA molecules that originated from bacteria), viruses, and yeast cells. Plasmids are not a part of the main cellular genome, but they can carry genes that provide the host cell with useful properties, such as drug resistance, mating ability, and toxin production. They are small enough to be conveniently manipulated experimentally, and, furthermore, they will carry extra DNA that is spliced into them.

CREATING THE CLONE

The steps in cloning are as follows. DNA is extracted from the organism under study and is cut into small fragments of a size suitable for cloning. Most often this is achieved by cleaving the DNA with a restriction enzyme. Restriction enzymes are extracted from several different species and strains of bacteria, in which they act as defense mechanisms against viruses. They can be thought of as "molecular scissors," cutting the DNA at specific target sequences. The most useful restriction enzymes make staggered cuts; that is, they leave a single-stranded overhang at the site of cleavage. These overhangs are very useful in cloning because the unpaired nucleotides will pair with other overhangs made using the same restriction enzyme. So, if the donor DNA and the vector DNA are both

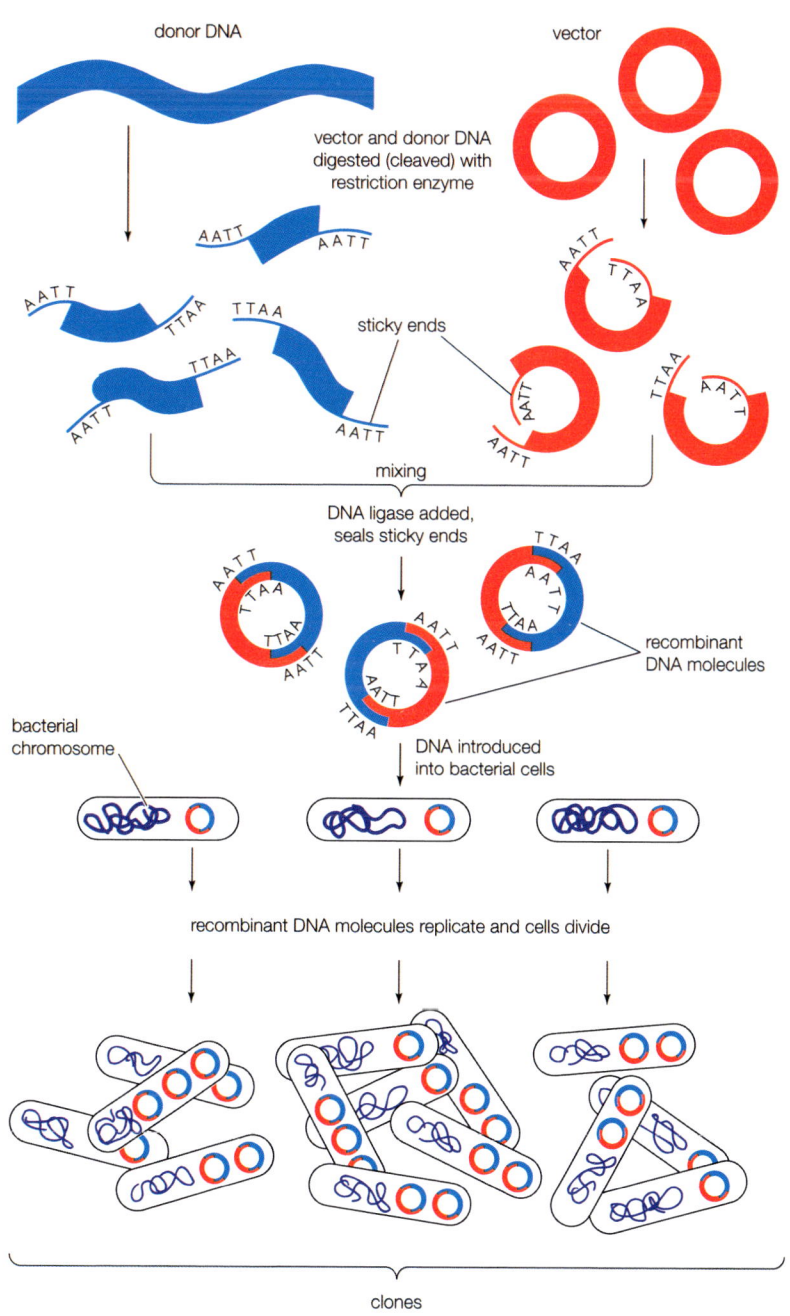

Steps involved in the engineering of a recombinant DNA molecule.

cut with the same enzyme, there is a strong possibility that the donor fragments and the cut vector will splice together because of the complementary overhangs. The resulting molecule is called recombinant DNA. It is recombinant in the sense that it is composed of DNA from two different sources. Thus, it is a type of DNA that would be impossible naturally and is an artifact created by DNA technology.

The next step in the cloning process is to cut the vector with the same restriction enzyme used to cut the donor DNA. Vectors have target sites for many different restriction enzymes, but the most convenient ones are those that occur only once in the vector molecule. This is because the restriction enzyme then merely opens up the vector ring, creating a space for the insertion of the donor DNA segment. Cut vector DNA and donor DNA are mixed in a test tube, and the complementary ends of both types of DNA unite randomly. Of course, several types of unions are possible: donor fragment to donor fragment, vector fragment to vector fragment, and, most important, vector fragment to donor fragment, which can be selected for. Recombinant DNA associations form spontaneously in the above manner, but these associations are not stable because, although the ends are paired, the sugar-phosphate backbone of the DNA has not been sealed. This is accomplished by the application of an enzyme called

DNA ligase, which seals the two segments, forming a continuous and stable double helix.

The mixture should now contain a population of vectors each containing a different donor insert. This solution is mixed with live bacterial cells that have been specially treated to make their cells more permeable to DNA. Recombinant molecules enter living cells in a process called transformation. Usually, only a single recombinant molecule will enter any individual bacterial cell. Once inside, the recombinant DNA molecule replicates like any other plasmid DNA molecule, and many copies are subsequently produced. Furthermore, when the bacterial cell divides, all of the daughter cells receive the recombinant plasmid, which again replicates in each daughter cell.

The original mixture of transformed bacterial cells is spread out on the surface of a growth medium in a flat dish (Petri dish) so that the cells are separated from one another. These individual cells are invisible to the naked eye, but as each cell undergoes successive rounds of cell division, visible colonies form. Each colony is a cell clone, but it is also a DNA clone because the recombinant vector has now been amplified by replication during every round of cell division. Thus, the Petri dish, which may contain many hundreds of distinct colonies, represents a large number of clones of different DNA fragments. This collection of clones is called a DNA library. By considering the size of the

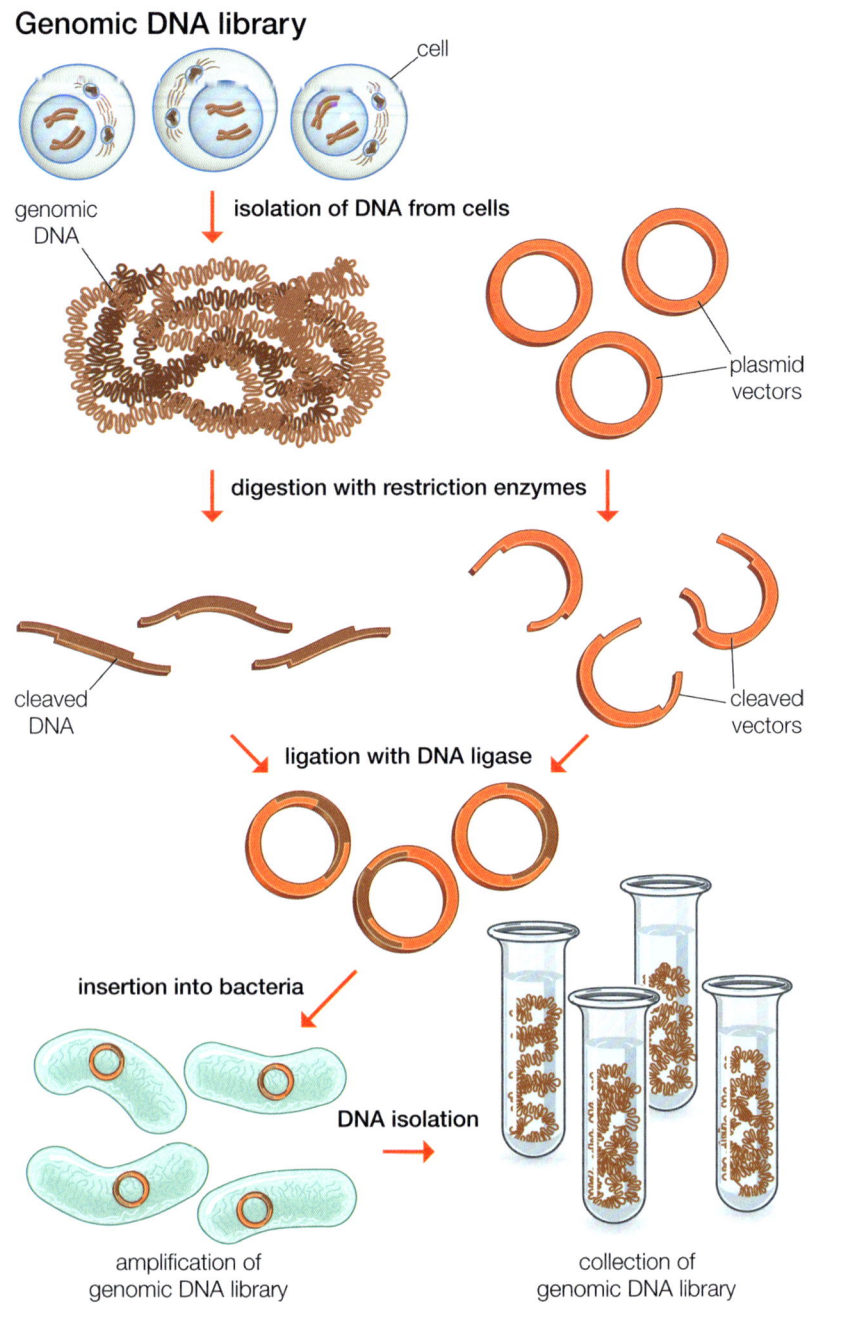

A genomic DNA library is a collection of DNA fragments that make up the full-length genome of an organism. A genomic library is created by isolating DNA from cells and then amplifying it using DNA cloning technology.

GENE THERAPY

donor genome and the average size of the inserts in the recombinant DNA molecule, a researcher can calculate the number of clones needed to encompass the entire donor genome, or, in other words, the number of clones needed to constitute a genomic library.

VECTORS

Several bacterial viruses have also been used as vectors. The most commonly used is the lambda phage. The central part of the lambda genome is not essential for the virus to replicate in *Escherichia coli*, so this can be excised using an appropriate restriction enzyme, and inserts from donor DNA can be spliced into the gap. In fact, when the phage repackages DNA into its protein capsule, it includes only DNA fragments the same length of the normal phage genome.

Vectors are chosen depending on the total amount of DNA that must be included in a library. Cosmids are engineered vectors that are hybrids of plasmid and phage lambda; however, they can carry larger inserts than either pUC plasmids (plasmids engineered to produce a very high number of DNA copies but that can accommodate only small inserts) or lambda phage alone. Bacterial artificial chromosomes (BACs) are vectors based on F-factor (fertility factor) plasmids of *E. coli* and can carry much larger amounts of DNA. Yeast artificial chromosomes (YACs) are vectors based on autonomously replicating plasmids of *Saccharomyces cerevisiae* (baker's yeast). In yeast (a eukaryotic organism) a YAC behaves like a yeast chromosome and segregates properly into daughter cells. These vectors can carry the largest inserts of all and are used extensively in cloning large genomes such as the human genome.

ISOLATING THE CLONE

In general, cloning is undertaken in order to obtain the clone of one particular gene or DNA sequence of interest. The next step after cloning, therefore, is to find and isolate that clone among other members of the library. If the library encompasses the whole genome of an organism, then somewhere within that library will be the desired clone. There are several ways of finding it, depending on the specific gene concerned. Most commonly, a cloned DNA segment that shows homology to the sought gene is used as a probe. For example, if a mouse gene has already been cloned, then that clone can be used to find the equivalent human clone from a human genomic library. Bacterial colonies constituting a library are grown in a collection of Petri dishes. Then a porous membrane is laid over the surface of each plate, and cells adhere to the membrane. The cells are ruptured, and DNA is separated into single strands—all on the membrane. The probe is also separated into single strands and labeled, often with radioactive phosphorus. A solution of the

GENE THERAPY

radioactive probe is then used to bathe the membrane. The single-stranded probe DNA will adhere only to the DNA of the clone that contains the equivalent gene. The membrane is dried and placed against a sheet of radiation-sensitive film, and somewhere on the films a black spot will appear, announcing the presence and location of the desired clone. The clone can then be retrieved from the original Petri dishes.

REVERSE GENETICS

Recombinant DNA technology has made possible a type of genetics called reverse genetics. Traditionally, genetic research starts with a mutant phenotype, and, by Mendelian crossing analysis, a researcher is able to attribute the phenotype to a specific gene. Reverse genetics travels in precisely the opposite direction. Researchers begin with a gene of unknown function and use molecular analysis to determine its phenotype. One important tool in reverse genetics is gene knockout. By mutating the cloned gene of unknown function and using it to replace the resident copy or copies, the resultant mutant phenotype will show which biological function this gene normally controls.

DIAGNOSTICS

Recombinant DNA technology has led to powerful diagnostic procedures useful in both medicine and

GENETIC TESTING AND GENE THERAPY

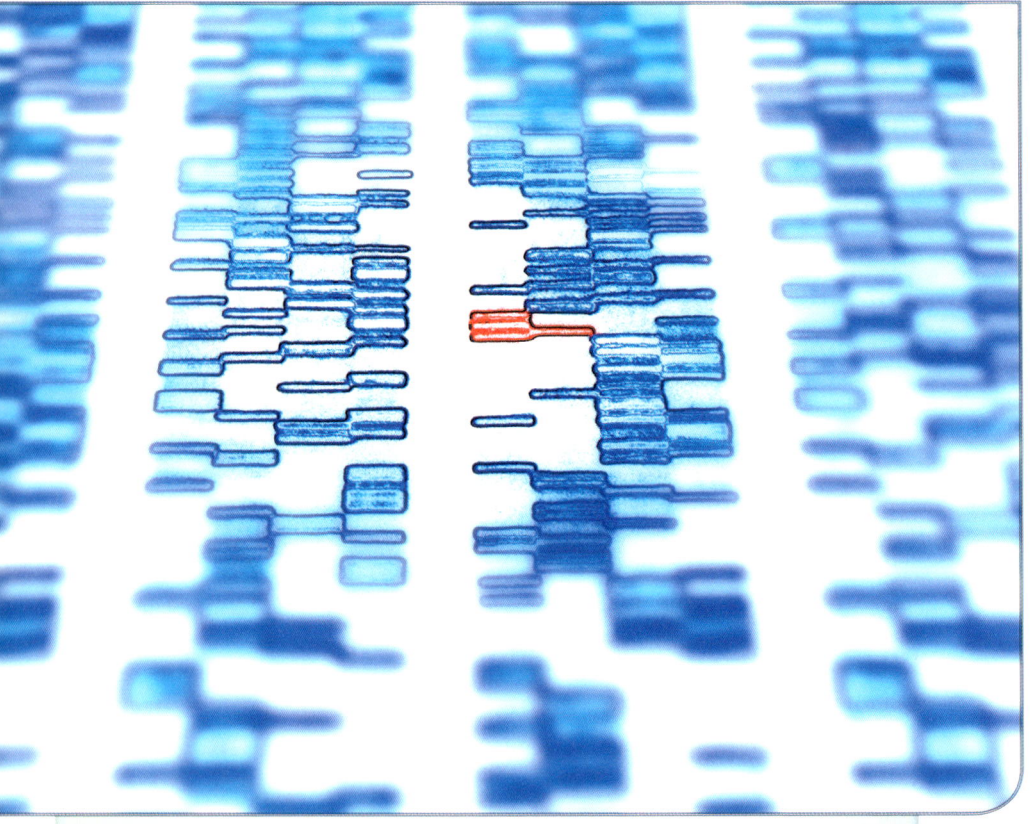

This is what is known as a DNA fingerprint.

forensics. In medicine these diagnostic procedures are used in counseling prospective parents as to the likelihood of having a child with a particular disease, and they are also used in the prenatal prediction of genetic disease in the fetus. Researchers look for specific DNA fragments that are located in close proximity to the gene that causes the disease of concern.

These fragments, called restriction fragment length polymorphisms (RFLPs), often serve as effective "genetic markers." In forensics, DNA fragments called variable number tandem repeats (VNTRs), which are highly variable between individuals, are employed to produce what is called a "DNA fingerprint." A DNA fingerprint can be used to determine if blood or other body fluids left at the scene of a crime belongs to a suspect.

GENOMICS

The genetic analysis of entire genomes is called genomics. Such a broadscale analysis has been made possible by the development of recombinant DNA technology. In humans, knowledge of the entire genome sequence has facilitated searching for genes that produce hereditary diseases. It is also capable of revealing a set of proteins—produced at specific times, in specific tissues, or in specific diseases—that might be targets for therapeutic drugs. Genomics also allows the comparison of one genome with another, leading to insights into possible evolutionary relationships between organisms.

Genomics has two subdivisions: structural genomics and functional genomics. Structural genomics is based on the complete nucleotide sequence of a genome. Each member of a library of clones is physically manipulated by robots and sequenced by automatic sequencing machines, enabling a very high throughput of DNA. The resulting sequences are then assembled by a computer into a complete sequence for every chromosome. The complete DNA sequence is scanned by computer to find the positions of open reading frames (ORFs), or prospective genes. The sequences are then compared to the sequences of known genes from other organisms, and possible functions are assigned. Some ORFs remain unassigned, awaiting further research.

Functional genomics attempts to understand function at the broadest level (the genomic level). In one approach, gene functions of as many ORFs as possible are assigned as above in an attempt to obtain a full set of proteins encoded by the genome (called a proteome). The proteome broadly defines all the cellular functions used by the organism. Function in relation to specific developmental stages also is assessed by trying to identify the "transcriptome," the set of mRNA transcripts made at specific developmental stages. The practical approach utilizes microarrays—glass plates the size of a microscope slide imprinted with tens of thousands of ordered DNA samples, each representing one gene (either a clone or a synthesized segment). The mRNA preparation under test is labeled with a fluorescent dye, and the microarray is bathed in this mRNA. Fluorescent spots appear on the array indicating which mRNAs were present, thus defining the transcriptome.

GENE THERAPY

PROTEIN MANUFACTURE

Recombinant DNA procedures have been used to convert bacteria into "factories" for the synthesis of foreign proteins. This technique is useful not only for preparing large amounts of protein for basic research but also for producing valuable proteins for medical use. For example, the genes for human proteins such as growth hormone, insulin, and blood-clotting factor can be commercially manufactured. Another approach to producing proteins via recombinant DNA technology is to introduce the desired gene into the genome of an animal, engineered in such a way that the protein is secreted in the animal's milk, facilitating harvesting.

A NEW APPROACH

Human gene therapy has been attempted on somatic (body) cells for diseases such as cystic fibrosis, adenosine deaminase deficiency, familial hypercholesterolemia, cancer, and severe combined immunodeficiency (SCID) syndrome. Somatic cells cured by gene therapy may reverse the symptoms of disease in the treated individual, but the modification is not passed on to the next generation. Germline gene therapy aims to place corrected cells inside the germ line (e.g., cells of the ovary or testis). If that is achieved, those cells will undergo meiosis and provide a normal gametic contribution to the next

GENE DOPING

Since the latter half of the 20th century, the manipulation of human genes has formed an important area of biomedical research. Much effort has focused in particular on refining gene therapy for the treatment of diseases. In the early 21st century, members of the international sports community became concerned that athletes seeking to gain physical advantage in competition would abuse gene therapy through a process known as gene doping.

In gene doping, substances or techniques are used to manipulate cells or genes in order to improve athletic performance. Repoxygen is one therapy with potential for such doping. It consists of a segment of DNA designed to stimulate the synthesis of erythropoietin to augment the production of red blood cells (erythrocytes). The DNA is packaged in a viral delivery system, enabling the foreign DNA to be transferred to host cells where it becomes integrated into the cells' own DNA. The gene insert then instructs cells to synthesize erythropoietin. Increased numbers of red cells expand the oxygen-carrying capacity of blood, improving aerobic capacity.

In 2003, although no athletes were known to have experimented with gene doping, the World Anti-Doping Agency, which regulates the use of substances in sports, added the transfer of cells, DNA, or RNA and the use of all other gene-altering agents, biological or pharmacological, to its list of prohibited substances and methods.

generation. Germline gene therapy has been achieved experimentally in animals but not in humans.

Scientists have also explored the possibility of combining gene therapy with stem cell therapy. In a preliminary test of that approach, scientists collected skin cells from a patient with alpha-1 antitrypsin deficiency (an inherited disorder associated with certain types of lung and liver disease), reprogrammed the cells into stem cells, corrected the causative gene mutation, and then stimulated the cells to mature into liver cells. The reprogrammed, genetically corrected cells functioned normally.

SOMATIC CELL NUCLEAR TRANSFER

Following experiments in animals, including those used to create Dolly the sheep, there has been much discussion about the use of somatic cell nuclear transfer (SCNT) to create pluripotent human cells. In SCNT the nucleus of a somatic cell (a fully differentiated cell, excluding germ cells), which contains the majority of the cell's DNA (deoxyribonucleic acid), is removed and transferred into an unfertilized egg cell that has had its own nuclear DNA removed. The egg cell is grown in culture until it reaches the blastocyst stage. The inner cell mass is then removed from the egg, and the cells are grown in culture to form an embryonic stem cell line (generations of cells

GENETIC TESTING AND GENE THERAPY

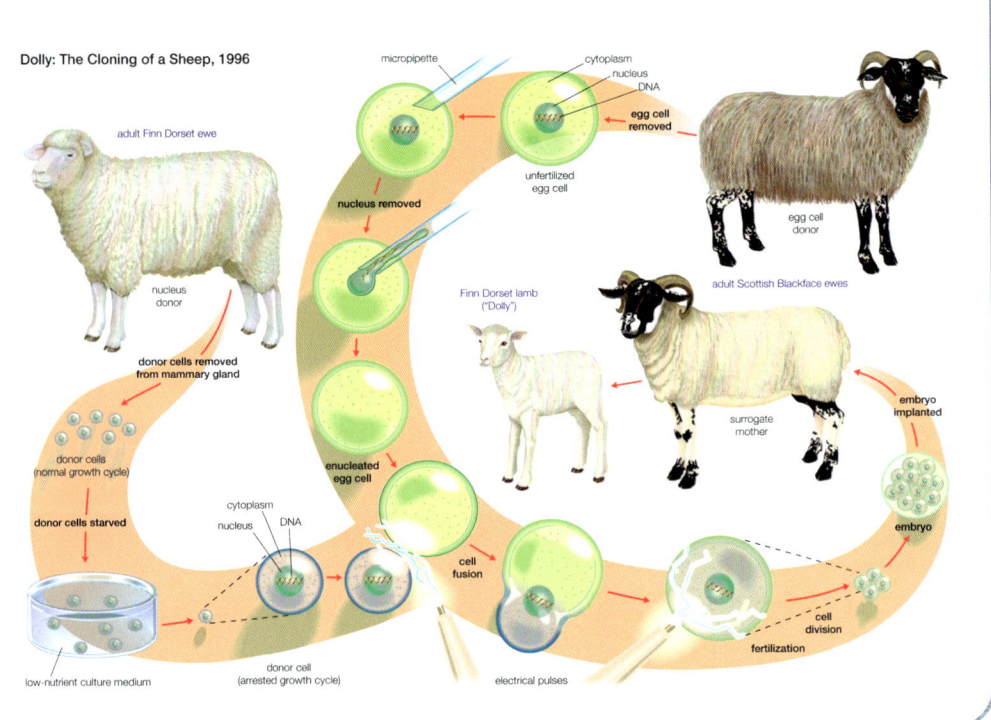

Dolly the sheep was cloned using the process of somatic cell nuclear transfer (SCNT).

originating from the same group of parent cells). These cells can then be stimulated to differentiate into various types of cells needed for transplantation. Since these cells would be genetically identical to the original donor, they could be used to treat the donor with no problems of immune rejection. Scientists generated human embryonic stem cells successfully from SCNT human embryos for the first time in 2013.

GENE THERAPY

While promising, the generation and use of SCNT-derived embryonic stem cells is controversial for several reasons. One is that SCNT can require more than a dozen eggs before one egg successfully produces embryonic stem cells. Human eggs are in short supply, and there are many legal and ethical problems associated with egg donation. There are also unknown risks involved with transplanting SCNT-derived stem cells into humans, because the mechanism by which the unfertilized egg is able to reprogram the nuclear DNA of a differentiated cell is not entirely understood. In addition, SCNT is commonly used to produce clones of animals (such as Dolly). Although the cloning of humans is currently illegal throughout the world, the egg cell that contains nuclear DNA from an adult cell could in theory be implanted into a woman's uterus and come to term as an actual cloned human. Thus, there exists strong opposition among some groups to the use of SCNT to generate human embryonic stem cells.

Induced pluripotent stem cells

Due to the ethical and moral issues surrounding the use of embryonic stem cells, scientists have searched for ways to reprogram adult somatic cells. Studies of cell fusion, in which differentiated adult somatic cells grown in culture with embryonic stem cells fuse with the stem cells and acquire embryonic stem-cell-like properties, led to the idea that specific genes could reprogram differentiated adult cells. An advantage of cell fusion is that it relies on existing embryonic stem cells instead of eggs. However, fused cells stimulate an immune response when transplanted into humans, which leads to transplant rejection. As a result, research has become increasingly focused on the genes and proteins capable of reprogramming adult cells to a pluripotent state.

In order to make adult cells pluripotent without fusing them to embryonic stem cells, regulatory genes that induce pluripotency must be introduced into the nuclei of adult cells. To do this, adult cells are grown in cell culture, and specific combinations of regulatory genes are inserted into retroviruses (viruses that convert RNA [ribonucleic acid] into DNA), which are then introduced to the culture medium. The retroviruses transport the RNA of the regulatory genes into the nuclei of the adult cells, where the genes are then incorporated into the DNA of the cells. About 1 out of every 10,000 cells acquires embryonic stem cell properties. Although the mechanism is still uncertain, it is clear that some of the genes confer embryonic stem cell properties by means of the regulation of numerous other genes. Adult cells that become reprogrammed in this way are known as induced pluripotent stem cells (iPS).

INDUCED PLURIPOTENT STEM CELLS

Similar to embryonic stem cells, induced pluripotent stem cells can be stimulated to differentiate into select types of cells that could in principle be used for disease-specific treatments. In addition, the generation of induced pluripotent stem cells from the adult cells of patients affected by genetic diseases can be used to model the diseases in the laboratory. For example, in 2008 researchers isolated skin cells from a child with an inherited neurological disease called spinal muscular atrophy and then reprogrammed these cells into induced pluripotent stem cells. The reprogrammed cells retained the disease genotype of the adult cells and were stimulated to differentiate into motor neurons that displayed functional insufficiencies associated with spinal muscular atrophy. By recapitulating the disease in the laboratory, scientists were able to study closely the cellular changes that occurred as the disease progressed. Such models promise not only to improve scientists' understanding of genetic diseases but also to facilitate the development of new therapeutic strategies tailored to each type of genetic disease.

In 2009 scientists successfully generated retinal cells of the human eye by reprogramming adult skin cells. This advance enabled detailed investigation of the embryonic development of retinal cells and opened avenues for the generation of novel therapies for eye diseases. The production of retinal cells from reprogrammed skin cells may be particularly useful in the treatment of retinitis pigmentosa, which is characterized by the progressive degeneration of the retina, eventually leading to night blindness and other complications of vision. Although retinal cells also have been produced from human embryonic stem cells, induced pluripotency represents a less controversial approach. Scientists have also explored the possibility of combining induced pluripotent stem cell technology with gene therapy, which would be of value particularly for patients with genetic disease who would benefit from autologous transplantation.

Researchers have also been able to generate cardiac stem cells for the treatment of certain forms of heart disease through the process of dedifferentiation, in which mature heart cells are stimulated to revert to stem cells. The first attempt at the transplantation of autologous cardiac stem cells was performed in 2009, when doctors isolated heart tissue from a patient, cultured the tissue in a laboratory, stimulated cell dedifferentiation, and then reinfused the cardiac stem cells directly into the patient's heart. A similar study involving 14 patients who underwent cardiac bypass surgery followed by cardiac stem cell transplantation was reported in 2011. More than three months after stem cell transplantation, the patients experienced a slight but detectable improvement in heart function.

Patient-specific induced pluripotent stem cells and dedifferentiated cells are highly valuable in terms of their therapeutic applications because they are unlikely to be rejected by the immune system. However, before induced pluripotent stem cells can be used to treat human diseases, researchers must find a way to introduce the active reprogramming genes without using retroviruses, which can cause diseases such as leukemia in humans. A possible alternative to the use of retroviruses to transport regulatory genes into the nuclei of adult cells is the use of plasmids, which are less tumourigenic than viruses.

CHAPTER 5
BIOETHICAL CONSIDERATIONS

Some aspects of gene therapy, including genetic manipulation and selection, research on embryonic tissue, and experimentation on human subjects, have aroused ethical controversy and safety concerns. Some objections to gene therapy are based on the view that humans should not "play God" and interfere in the natural order. On the other hand, others have argued that genetic engineering may be justified where it is consistent with the purposes of God as creator. Some critics are particularly concerned about the safety of germline gene therapy, because any harm caused by such treatment could be passed to successive generations—generations without a say in the decision to alter the germline. Benefits, however, would also be passed on indefinitely. There also has been concern that the use of somatic gene therapy may affect germ cells. Bioethics is the branch of applied ethics that studies the philosophical, social, and legal issues arising in medicine and the life sciences. It is chiefly concerned with human life and well-being, though it sometimes also treats ethical questions relating to the nonhuman biological environment.

BIOETHICS

The range of issues considered to fall within the purview of bioethics varies depending on how broadly the field is defined. In one common usage, bioethics is more or less equivalent to medical ethics, or biomedical ethics. The term "medical ethics" itself has been challenged, however, in light of the growing interest in issues dealing with health care professions other than medicine, in particular nursing. The professionalization of nursing and the perception of nurses as ethically accountable in their own right has led to the development of a distinct field known as nursing ethics. Accordingly, "health care ethics" has come into use as a more inclusive term. Bioethics, however, is broader than this, because some of the issues it encompasses concern not so much the practice of health care as the conduct and results of research in the life sciences, especially in areas such as cloning and gene therapy, stem cell research, xenotransplantation (animal-to-human transplantation), and human longevity.

Painted portrait of Hippocrates.

BIOETHICAL CONSIDERATIONS

Although bioethics—and indeed the whole field of applied ethics as currently understood—is a fairly recent phenomenon, there have been discussions of moral issues in medicine since ancient times. Examples include the corpus of the Greek physician Hippocrates (460–377 BCE), after whom the Hippocratic oath is named (though Hippocrates himself was not its author); the *Republic* of Plato (428/27–348/47 BCE), which advocates selective human breeding in anticipation of later programs of eugenics; the *Summa contra gentiles* of St. Thomas Aquinas (1224/25–1274), which briefly discusses the permissibility of abortion; and the *Lectures on Ethics* of the German Enlightenment philosopher Immanuel Kant (1724-1804), which contains arguments against the sale of human body parts.

Bioethics emerged as a distinct field of study in the early 1960s. It was influenced not only by advances in the life sciences, particularly medicine, but also by the significant cultural and societal changes taking place at the time, primarily in the West. The perfection of certain lifesaving procedures and technologies, such as organ transplantation and kidney dialysis, required medical officials to make difficult decisions about which patients would receive treatment and which would be allowed to die. At the same time, the increasing importance placed on individual well-being contributed to changes in conventional attitudes toward marriage and sexuality, reproduction

GENETIC TESTING AND GENE THERAPY

and child rearing, and civil rights. The ultimate result was widespread dissatisfaction with traditional medical paternalism and the gradual recognition of a patient's right to be fully informed about his condition and to retain some measure of control over what happens to his body.

Increasingly, however, biological and medical ethics confronts problems that extend beyond the isolated, individual physician-patient relationship. The ethics of research on human subjects is one such example. A related issue is to what extent the tissues of aborted fetuses may be used in medical research. Many ethical problems also surround the use of alternative means of achieving pregnancy—surrogate parenting and artificial insemination using donor sperm, for example. Problems of public health is another area of ethical controversy—whether, for instance, to quarantine certain individuals in danger of spreading a disease in order to protect others, or whether to force people to take treatments such as vaccinations and fluorides in their water supply.

A major new area of bioethics is the ethics of health policy and health-resource allocation. Typical ethical problems faced by health planners include whether people have a right to health care and whether society has a right to force people into healthful behavior when it must pay for their care if they become ill. The most basic health-planning ethical problem is balancing the efficient use of health-care resources against a more equitable distribution even when less good is done in total. If efficiency is the dominant goal, some who have rare diseases, who live in out-of-the-way places, or who are members of minority groups will probably go untreated.

THE HIPPOCRATIC OATH

The Hippocratic Oath is an ethical code attributed to the ancient Greek physician Hippocrates (c. 400 BC). It has been adopted as a guide to conduct by the medical profession and is still used in the graduation ceremonies of many medical schools. Although little is known of the life of Hippocrates—or, indeed, if he was the only practitioner of the time using this name—a body of manuscripts, called the Hippocratic Collection (Corpus Hippocraticum), survived until modern times. In addition to containing information on medical matters, the collection embodied a code of principles for the teachers of medicine and for their students. This code, or a fragment of it, has been handed down in various versions through generations of physicians.

In the oath, the physician pledges to prescribe only beneficial treatments, according to his abilities and judgment; to refrain from causing harm or hurt; and to live an exemplary personal and professional life. At the most basic level, those taking the Hippocratic oath vow first, to do no harm. Ethical questions arise when one party in a decision does not have a voice in that decision, leaving that person to live with the consequences of the actions of others.

ISSUES IN BIOETHICS

One area of ethical concern is the area of eugenics. Eugenics is the selection of desired heritable characteristics in order to improve future generations, typically in reference to humans. The term "eugenics" was coined in 1883 by the British explorer and natural scientist Francis Galton, who, influenced by Charles Darwin's theory of natural selection, advocated a system that would allow "the more suitable races or strains of blood a better chance of prevailing speedily over the less suitable." Social Darwinism, the popular theory in the late 19th century that life for humans in society was ruled by "survival of the fittest," helped advance eugenics into serious scientific study in the early 1900s. By World War I, many scientific authorities and political leaders supported eugenics. However, it ultimately failed as a science in the 1930s and '40s, when the assumptions of eugenicists became heavily criticized and the Nazis used eugenics to support the extermination of entire races.

Despite the dropping of the term "eugenics," eugenic ideas remain prevalent in many issues surrounding human reproduction. Medical genetics, a post-World War II medical specialty, encompasses a wide range of health concerns, from genetic screening and counseling to fetal gene manipulation and the treatment of adults suffering from hereditary disorders. Because certain diseases (e.g., hemophilia

BIOETHICAL CONSIDERATIONS

Eugenics, the selection of desired heritable characteristics in order to improve future generations, is a bioethical concern.

GENETIC TESTING AND GENE THERAPY

and Tay-Sachs disease) are now known to be genetically transmitted, many couples choose to undergo genetic screening, in which they learn the chances that their offspring have of being affected by some combination of their hereditary backgrounds. Couples at risk of passing on genetic defects may opt to remain childless or to adopt children. Furthermore, it is now possible to diagnose certain genetic defects in the unborn. Many couples choose to terminate a pregnancy that involves a genetically disabled offspring. These developments have reinforced the eugenic aim of identifying and eliminating undesirable genetic material. Counterbalancing this trend, however, has been medical progress that enables victims of many genetic diseases to live fairly normal lives. Direct manipulation of harmful genes is also being studied. If perfected, it could obviate eugenic arguments for restricting reproduction among those who carry harmful genes. Such conflicting innovations have complicated the controversy surrounding what many call the "new eugenics." Moreover, suggestions for expanding eugenics programs, which range from the creation of sperm banks for the genetically superior to the potential cloning of human beings, have met with vigorous resistance from the public, which often views such programs as unwarranted interference with nature or as opportunities for abuse by authoritarian regimes.

    Scientists are rapidly developing the capacity to go beyond aborting fetuses with genetic defects.

BIOETHICAL CONSIDERATIONS

They are learning how to change genetic material, how to move genes from one species to another, and how to replace a defective gene with a more normal one. When this technology is perfected, it may have crucial effects on agriculture, production of livestock, and production of drugs as well as providing the potential to replace defective genes in humans. While the benefits are potentially enormous, objections are also being raised. These include concern that new species of microorganisms, for example, may be created that could cause uncontrollable disease or some serious, unexpected harm. The most fundamental question raised by this new work is whether there is something basically unethical about human attempts to change genetic codes to create new species of animals.

Applications of the Human Genome Project are often referred to as "Brave New World" genetics or the "new eugenics"; however, the ethical, legal, and social implications of this international project are monitored much more closely than were early 20th-century eugenics programs. Still, with or without the use of the term, many eugenics-related concerns are reemerging as a new group of individuals decide how to regulate the application of genetics science and technology. This gene-directed activity, in attempting to improve upon nature, may not be that distant from what Galton implied in 1909 when he described eugenics as the "study of agencies, under social control, which may improve or impair" future generations.

THE HEALTH CARE CONTEXT

The issues studied in bioethics can be grouped into several categories. One category concerns the relationship between doctor and patient, including issues that arise from conflicts between a doctor's duty to promote the health of his patient and the patient's right to self-determination or autonomy, a right that in the medical context is usually taken to encompass a right to be fully informed about one's condition and a right to be consulted about the course of one's treatment. Is a doctor obliged to tell a patient that he is terminally ill if there is good reason to believe that doing so would hasten the patient's death? If a patient with a life-threatening illness refuses treatment, should his wishes be respected? Should patients always be permitted to refuse the use of extraordinary life-support measures? These questions become more complicated when the patient is incapable of making rational decisions in his own interest, as in the case of infants and children, patients suffering from disabling psychiatric disorders such as schizophrenia or degenerative brain diseases such as Alzheimer disease, and patients who are in a vegetative state.

Many of the moral issues that have arisen in the health care context and in the wake of advances in

BIOETHICAL CONSIDERATIONS

medical technology have been addressed, in whole or in part, in legislation. It is important to realize, however, that the content of such legislation is seldom, if ever, dictated by the positions one takes on particular moral issues. For example, the view that voluntary euthanasia is morally permissible in certain circumstances does not by itself settle the question of whether euthanasia should be legalized. The possibility of legalization carries with it another set of issues, such as the potential for abuse. Some bioethicists have expressed the concern that the legalization of euthanasia would create a perception among some elderly patients that society expects them to request euthanasia, even if they do not desire it, in order not to be a burden to others. Similarly, even those who believe that abortion is morally permissible in certain circumstances may consistently object to proposals to relax or eliminate laws against it.

TRADITIONAL PHILOSOPHICAL QUESTIONS

Another category of issues concerns a host of philosophical questions about the definition and significance of life and death, the nature of personhood and identity, and the extent of human freedom and individual responsibility. At what point should a fatally injured or terminally ill patient be considered dead? When his vital functions—e.g., heartbeat and breathing—have ceased?

GENETIC TESTING AND GENE THERAPY

When the brain stem has ceased to function? Should the presence of deep coma be sufficient to establish death? These and similar questions were given new urgency in the 1960s, when the increased demand for human organs and tissues for use in transplant operations forced medical ethicists to establish guidelines for determining when it is permissible to remove organs from a potential donor.

At about the same time, the development of safer techniques of surgical abortion and the growing acceptability of abortion as a method of birth control prompted increasing debate about the moral status of the human fetus. In philosophical discussion, this debate was framed in terms of the notion of a "person," understood as any being whose interests are deserving of special moral concern. The central issue was whether—and, if so, at what stage—the fetus is a person in the moral sense. In slightly different terms, the issue was whether the class of persons is coextensive with the class of human beings—whether all and only human beings are persons, or whether instead there can be human beings who are not persons or persons who are not human beings (the latter category, according to some, includes some of the higher animals and hypothetical creatures such as intelligent Martians). These questions were raised anew in later decades in response to the development of drugs, such as RU-486 (mifepristone), that induce abortion up to several weeks after conception and to the use

BIOETHICAL CONSIDERATIONS

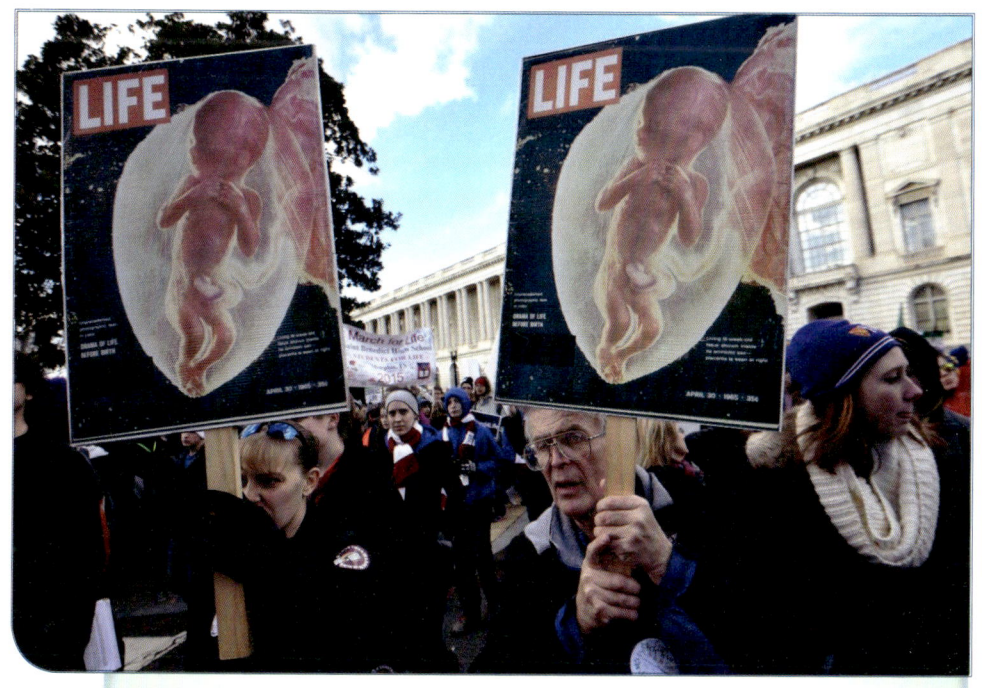

Abortion remains a hot-button issue in the United States.

of stem cells taken from human embryos in research on the treatment of conditions such as parkinsonism (Parkinson disease) and injuries of the central nervous system.

A closely related set of issues concerns the nature of personal identity. Recent advances in techniques of cloning, which enabled the successful cloning of animals such as sheep and rabbits, have renewed discussion of the traditional philosophical question of what, if anything, makes a particular human being the unique person he is. Is a person just the sum of the information encoded in his genes? If so, is the patient who has undergone gene therapy a different person from the one he was before—i.e., has he become someone else? If a human being were to be cloned, in what sense would he be a copy of his "parent"? Would he and his parent be the same person? If multiple human beings were cloned from the same parent, would they and their parent all be the same person?

The attempt to understand personal identity in terms of genetic information also raised anew the philosophical problems of free will and determinism. To what extent, if any, is human personality or character genetically rather than environmentally determined? Are there genetic bases for certain types of behaviour, as there seem to be for certain types of diseases (e.g., Tay-Sachs disease)? If so, what kinds of behaviour are so influenced, and to what extent are they also influenced by environmental factors? If behaviour is at least partly genetically determined, should individuals always be held fully responsible for what they do?

Finally, the possibility of developing technologies that would extend the human life span far beyond its current natural length, if not indefinitely, has led to speculation about the value of life, the significance of death, and the desirability of immortality. Is life intrinsically valuable? In cases in which one is not suffering

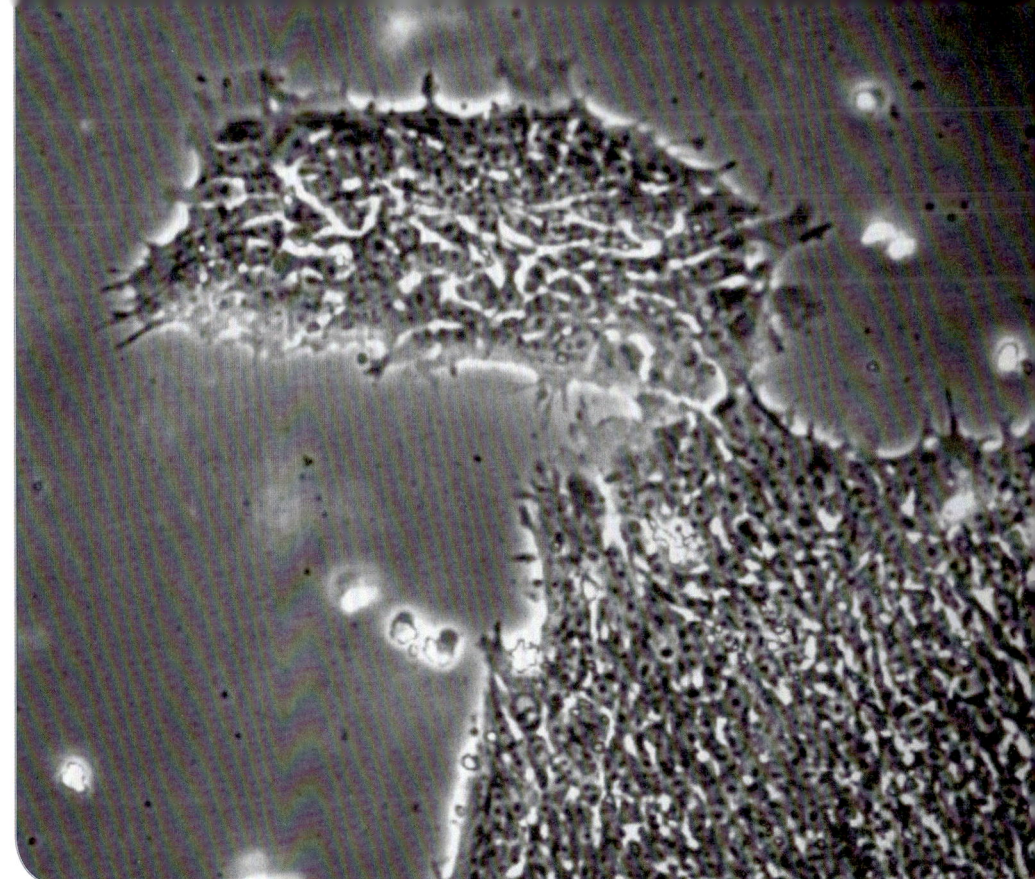

In 2009 President Obama signed an order reversing previous limits on human embryonic stem cell research. This allowed scientists to seek federal funding for their research in the use of stem cells to cure disease.

physically or emotionally, is it always better to be alive than dead? If so, is it rational to desire immortality? What would be the significance of death in a world in which dying was not biologically inevitable?

SOCIAL AND LEGAL ISSUES

Many of these philosophical questions, however they are answered, have significant social and legal dimensions. For example, advances in medical technology have the potential to create disproportionate disadvantages for some social groups, either by being applied in ways that harm members of the groups directly or by encouraging the adoption of social policies that discriminate unfairly against them. Accordingly, questions of discrimination in bioethics have arisen in a number of areas. In one such area, reproductive medicine, recently developed techniques have enabled parents to choose the sex of their child. Should this new power be considered liberating or oppressive? Would it be viewed positively if the vast majority of the parents who use it choose to have a boy rather than a girl? Similar concerns have been raised about the increasing use of abortion as a method of birth control in overpopulated countries such as India and China, where there is considerable social and legal pressure to limit family size and where male children are valued more highly than female children.

In the field of genetics, the use of relatively simple tests for determining a patient's susceptibility to certain genetically transmitted diseases has led to concerns in the United States and other countries that the results of such tests, if not properly safeguarded, could be used in unfair ways by health-insurance companies, employers, and government agencies. In addition, the advent of so-called "genetic counseling"—in which prospective parents receive advice about the chances that their offspring will inherit a certain genetic disease or

BIOETHICAL CONSIDERATIONS

disorder—has allowed couples to make more-informed decisions about reproduction but also has contributed, in the view of some bioethicists, to a social atmosphere considerably less tolerant of disability than it ought to be. The same criticism has been leveled against the practice of diagnosing, and in some cases treating, congenital defects in unborn children.

Persons who are affected by genetic disorders may find the concept of genetic counseling to be confrontational, inappropriate, or part of an eradication process. Societal investment in diagnostic technology and screening programs sends a message that disability is a major problem that should be prevented at all costs. The language of "risk," "abnormality," "burden," and "medical tragedy" may be viewed by disabled people as prejudiced, especially since it ignores the high quality of life that many disabled people achieve.

The aim of genetic counseling sessions for disabled persons often is the same as for individuals without disabilities. But disabled persons who choose not to have children may feel that they are somehow validating society's view or belief that their own lives are not valuable or worth living. Deciding whether or not to take the risk of passing on a genetic condition can be challenging to a disabled person's sense of self, raising problematic emotions. A genetic counselor should be able to provide such clients with accurate, balanced, and understandable information; help them to explore their feelings about possible outcomes;

and, most important, support the counselees through whatever choice they make.

Since the 1990s, genetic counselors' stated aspiration to provide nondirective counseling has been debated, and some observers have questioned whether nondirective counseling is achievable. They argue that the language in which counselors present risks and the information they provide about disability are bound to influence counselees' decision making. In practice, counselees often look to genetic counselors for direction, asking, in essence, "What would you do in this situation?" Genetic counselors must be able to support counselees regardless of the latter's decision. Thus, counselors need to have a heightened awareness of their own prejudices and moral stands on issues surrounding genetics and disability.

Research on the genetic bases of behaviour, though still in its infancy, is controversial, and it has even been criticized as scientifically invalid. Whatever its scientific merits, however, it has the potential, according to some bioethicists, to encourage the adoption of crude models of genetic determinism in the development of social policies, especially in the areas of education and crime prevention. Such policies, it is claimed, could result in unfair discrimination against large numbers of people judged to be genetically disposed to "undesirable" forms of behaviour, such as aggression or violence.

This last point suggests a related set of issues concerning the moral status of scientific inquiry

BIOETHICAL CONSIDERATIONS

itself. The notion that there is a clear line between, on the one hand, the discovery and presentation of scientific facts and, on the other, the discussion of moral issues—the idea that moral issues arise only after scientific research is concluded—is now widely regarded as mistaken. Science is not value-neutral. Indeed, there have been ethical debates about whether certain kinds of research should be undertaken at all, irrespective of their possible applications. It has been argued, for example, that research on the possible genetic basis of homosexuality is immoral, because even the assumption that such a basis exists implicitly characterizes homosexuality as a kind of genetic abnormality. In any case, it is plausible to suggest that scientific research should always be informed by philosophy—in particular by ethics but also, arguably, by the philosophy of mind. Consideration of the moral issues related to one particular branch of medicine, namely psychiatry, makes it clear that such issues arise not only in areas of treatment but also in matters of diagnosis and classification, where the application of labels indicating illness or abnormality may create serious disadvantages for the individuals so designated.

Virtually all groups recognize that there are some treatments available to dying patients that need not be given. Two criteria usually are used to identify treatments that are morally expendable: if they are useless or if they involve a grave burden. Traditionally it was left to the physician to decide if a treatment was

GENETIC TESTING AND GENE THERAPY

useless or burdensome. It is now widely held, especially among those who emphasize the rights of patients, that this judgment must be made by the patient because it should be based on the patient's own beliefs, values, and religious tradition. Thus, in the United States, an adult patient who is mentally competent is never forced by legal means to undergo treatment against his or her wishes (unless the treatment is for the benefit of another, such as

Right-to-die activist Dr. Jack Kevorkian was convicted for partaking in a physician-assisted suicide.

a vaccination or other public health measure). If the patient is not competent, the judgment must be made by a family member. If health professionals disagree strongly, they must seek a court order overturning the family member's judgment. This is done routinely, for example, in cases of parents who refuse a lifesaving blood transfusion for their child because of their religious beliefs.

A final class of social and legal questions concerns the allocation of health care resources. The issue of whether health care should be primarily an individual or a public responsibility remains deeply controversial. Although systems of health care allocation differ widely, they all face the problem that resources are scarce and consequently expensive. Debate has focused not only on the relative cost-effectiveness of different systems but also on the different conceptions of justice that underlie them. The global allocation of health care resources, including generic forms of drugs for life-threatening illnesses such as HIV/AIDS, is an important topic in the field of developing world bioethics.

TRADITIONAL AND CONTEMPORARY ETHICAL THEORIES

As a branch of applied ethics, bioethics is distinct from both metaethics, the study of basic moral concepts such as ought and good, and normative ethics, the discipline

GENETIC TESTING AND GENE THERAPY

SAVIOUR SIBLINGS

A saviour sibling is a child that is conceived to meet the genetic needs of an existing child in a family. It is the primary purpose of the saviour sibling to provide the genetic material essential to the survival of the existing child. To ensure that this is the case, genetic testing is done at the preimplantation stage of embryonic development. Only those embryos meeting the stated criteria will be treated as viable.

There are several ethical concerns cited with this practice. One is that the saviour sibling is not able to be party to the decision to act as the savior to the existing child. Another is that creating a child for the primary purpose of creating genetic material goes beyond simply having another child and hoping for a genetically favorably outcome, rising to the level of playing God and manipulating "destiny."

Jack and Linda Nash had their baby boy in order to save the life of their daughter, who was born with a rare genetic disease.

> Some involved in the ethical discussion argue that if the family were going to have another child, why not have that child assume this role. Others involved in the ethical discussion argue that selecting for a set of criteria that is beneficial to an existing child outweighs the fact that the family would have gone on to have another child.

that seeks to establish criteria for determining what kinds of action are morally right or wrong. To say that bioethics is "applied," however, does not imply that it presupposes any particular ethical theory. Contemporary bioethicists make use of a variety of different views, including primarily utilitarianism and Kantianism but also more recently developed perspectives such as virtue theory and perspectives drawn from philosophical feminism, particularly the school of thought known as the ethics of care.

Utilitarianism is a normative-ethical theory that holds that the moral rightness or wrongness of an action should be ascertained in terms of the action's consequences. According to one common formulation, an action is right if it would promote a greater amount of happiness for a greater number of people than would any other action performable in the same circumstances. The Kantian tradition, in contrast, eschews the notion of consequences and urges instead that an action is right only if it is universalizable—i.e., only if the moral rule it embodies could become a universal law applicable to all moral agents. The Kantian approach emphasizes respect for the individual, autonomy, dignity, and human rights.

Unlike these traditional approaches, both virtue ethics and the ethics of care focus on dimensions of moral theorizing other than determining the rightness or wrongness of particular actions. Virtue ethics is concerned with the nature of moral character and with the traits, capacities, or dispositions that moral agents ought to cultivate in themselves and others. Thus, the virtue ethicist may consider what character traits, such as compassion and courage, are desirable in a doctor, nurse, or biomedical researcher and how they would (or should) be manifested in various settings. The basic aim of the ethics of care is to replace—or at least augment—the supposedly "masculine" moral values of rationality, abstraction, impartiality, and independence with ostensibly more "feminine" values, such as emotion (particularly compassion and benevolence), particularity, partiality, and interdependence. From this perspective, reflection on abortion would begin not with abstract principles such as the right to autonomy or the right to life but with considerations of the needs of women who face the choice of whether to have an abortion and the particular ways in which their decisions may affect their lives and the lives of their families. This approach also would address social and legal aspects of the abortion debate, such as the fact that, though abortion affects the lives of women much more directly than it does the lives of men, women as a group are significantly underrepresented in the institutions that create abortion-related laws and regulations.

THE FOUR-PRINCIPLES APPROACH

Whereas some approaches in bioethics proceed by applying principles derived from independent ethical theories to individual cases (a "top-down" approach), others proceed by examining individual cases in order to elucidate the principles that seem to guide most people's thinking about bioethical issues in actual practice (a "bottom-up" approach). One very influential approach along these lines, known as the "four principles" of bioethics, attempts to describe a set of minimum moral conditions on the behaviour of health care professionals. The first principle, autonomy, entails that health care professionals should respect the autonomous decisions of competent adults. The second principle, beneficence, holds that they should aim to do good—i.e., to promote the interests of their patients. The third principle, nonmaleficence, requires that they should do no harm. Finally, the fourth principle, justice, holds that they should act fairly when the interests of different individuals or groups are in competition—e.g., by promoting the fair allocation of health care resources.

According to proponents of the four-principles approach, one of its advantages is that, because the principles are independent of any particular ethical theory, they can be used by theorists working in a variety of different traditions. Both the utilitarian and the Kantian, it is argued, can support the principle of autonomy, though they would do so for different reasons. Nevertheless, this adaptability may also be construed as a disadvantage. Critics have contended that the principles are so general that whatever agreement on them there may be is unlikely to be very meaningful. Thus, although the utilitarian and the Kantian may both accept the principle of autonomy, the principle as it is formulated allows them to understand the notion of autonomy in very different ways. Another criticism of the approach is that it does not offer any clear way of prioritizing between the principles in cases where they conflict—as they are often liable to do. The principle of autonomy, for example, might conflict with the principle of beneficence in cases where a competent adult patient refuses to accept life-saving treatment.

Despite these problems, the principles remain useful as a framework in which to think about moral issues in medicine and the life sciences. This is not an inconsiderable contribution, for, on at least one conception of the field, the main task of bioethics is not so much to provide answers to moral problems as to identify where the problems lie.

THE SIGNIFICANCE OF PUBLIC ATTITUDES

Since its inception the field of bioethics has been populated by specialists from a number of different disciplines, including primarily philosophers, lawyers, and theologians. In the last decade of the 20th century, however, the contributions of social scientists to bioethical research became particularly important. Work of this type involved surveys of public attitudes to advances in the life sciences, including xenotransplantation and genetic modification. Programs for facilitating public understanding of these advances were developed, leading to the establishment of "public understanding" and later "public engagement," or "participation," as distinct topics of study in bioethics and the social sciences.

These topics have been important from both a practical and a theoretical point of view. In order to formulate sound public policies on issues such as human cloning, for example, it is important to be able to predict how such technology, were it to become widely available, would affect the public's decision making about reproduction. At the same time, research on public attitudes may reveal that some bioethical principles, such as the principle of autonomy, may not be suitable for some societies, particularly those with cultures that are not particularly individualistic. For these societies, something like a "principle of solidarity" may have greater relevance. Nevertheless, it would be a mistake to assume that one of these principles must apply to the exclusion of the other—it is possible for a society to value both autonomy and solidarity.

POLICY MAKING

The importance of the social and legal issues addressed in bioethics is reflected in the large number of national and international bodies established to advise governments on appropriate public policy. At the national level, several countries have set up bioethics councils or commissions, including the President's Council on Bioethics in the United States, the Det Etiske Råd (Danish Council of Ethics) in Denmark, and the Comité Consultatif National d'Ethique (National Consultative Bioethics Committee) in France. Elsewhere, as in the United Kingdom, there are a variety of different bodies that consider bioethical issues. The Nuffield Council on Bioethics has taken on the role of a national bioethics committee to a certain extent, but there also are national bodies that deal with specific fields, such as the Human Genetics Commission.

Several international organizations also are involved in policy making on bioethical issues. The

United Nations Educational, Scientific and Cultural Organization (UNESCO), for example, has an International Bioethics Committee; the Human Genome Organisation has an Ethics Committee; and the Council of Europe has issued the Convention on Human Rights and Biomedicine. The proliferation of such committees is evidence of the increasing political influence of the work performed by bioethicists. Indeed, acquaintance with developments in bioethics arguably is becoming an important aspect of national and global citizenship. At the same time, however, the role of bioethical experts on advisory or decision-making bodies has itself become a topic of study in bioethics.

GLOBAL BIOETHICS

The field of bioethics has grown most rapidly in North America, Australia and New Zealand, and Europe. Cross-cultural discussion also has expanded and in 1992 led to the establishment of the International Association of Bioethics. A significant discussion under way at the start of the 21st century concerned the possibility of a "global" bioethics that would be capable of encompassing the values and cultural traditions of non-Western societies. Some bioethicists maintained that a global bioethics could be founded on the four-principles approach, in view of its apparent compatibility with widely differing ethical theories and worldviews. Others argued to the contrary that the four principles are not an appropriate basis for a global bioethics because at least some of them—in particular the principle of autonomy—reflect peculiarly Western values. Although the issue remains unresolved, the field as a whole continues to grow in sophistication. At the same time, the increasing pace of technological advances in medicine and the life sciences demands that bioethicists continually rethink the basic assumptions of their field and reflect carefully on their own methodologies.

Even as the field of bioethics matures in societies that currently have the capacity to alter the genetic composition of individuals, this ability will be introduced to additional societies. The way in which bioethical issues are handled on the local and global scale will greatly influence the effect of genetic testing and treatment upon future generations.

CONCLUSION

With each contribution to science, researchers provide another stepping stone for those who will follow. The invention of the microscope, the mapping of the human genome, and experimentation with DNA have all contributed to the field of genetic testing and gene therapy. The ability to work directly with the genetic material of human beings has led to a number of ethical considerations. It has also made it possible to alter the outcome for those with genetic diseases. As more countries are able to take part in this technology over the next decades, the roles played by genetic testing and gene therapy will be determined on a global scale. Whether it will lead to a brave new world filled with promise or one of blighted opportunity remains to be seen.

GLOSSARY

CHROMOSOMAL KARYOTYPING A genetic test in which chromosomes are arranged according to a standard classification scheme.

CHROMOSOME One of the usually rod-shaped or threadlike DNA-containing structures that contain all or most of the genes of an organism and that are located in the nucleus in eukaryotes and are usually ring-shaped in prokaryotes.

DEDIFFERENTIATION The process in which mature heart cells are stimulated to revert to stem cells.

EUGENICS The selection of desired heritable characteristics in order to improve future generations, typically in reference to humans.

FLUORESCENCE IN SITU HYBRIDIZATION (FISH) A technique used to identify structural abnormalities in chromosomes that standard tests such as karyotyping cannot detect.

GENE THERAPY The introduction of a normal gene into an individual's genome in order to repair a mutation that causes a genetic disease.

GENETICS A branch of biology that deals with heredity and variation of organisms.

GENOMICS The genetic analysis of entire genomes.

GENOTYPE The genetic constitution of an organism.

GERMLINE The cellular lineage of a sexually reproducing organism from which eggs and sperm are derived.

GLOSSARY

HEREDITY The sum of all biological processes by which particular characteristics are transmitted from parents to their offspring.

MEIOSIS The division of a germ cell involving two fissions of the nucleus and giving rise to four gametes, or sex cells, each possessing half the number of chromosomes of the original cell.

MITOSIS A process of cell duplication, or reproduction, during which one cell gives rise to two genetically identical daughter cells.

NANOSCALE Having dimensions usually measured in nanometers.

PEDIGREE A table or list showing the line of ancestors of an animal or person.

PHENOTYPE All the observable characteristics of an organism, such as shape, size, colour, and behaviour, that result from the interaction of its genotype (total genetic inheritance) with the environment.

PLEIOTROPY A condition wherein one gene may affect many traits.

PLURIPOTENT Capable of differentiating into one of many cell types.

PREIMPLANTATION GENETIC DIAGNOSIS (PGD) A procedure used to detect the presence of embryonic genetic abnormalities that have a high likelihood of causing implantation failure or miscarriage.

PROBAND The individual partaking in genetic counseling.

GENETIC TESTING AND GENE THERAPY

PROGENITOR A direct ancestor or originator.
RECOMBINANT DNA TECHNOLOGY Joining together of DNA molecules from two different species that are inserted into a host organism to produce new genetic combinations that are of value to science, medicine, agriculture, and industry.
SOMATIC CELL One of the cells of the body that compose the tissues, organs, and parts of an individual other than the germ cells.

BIBLIOGRAPHY

BIOETHICS

GENERAL

Helga Kuhse and Peter Singer (eds.), *A Companion to Bioethics* (1998), features reviews of key topics in the field.

ISSUES

Allen Buchanan et al., *From Chance to Choice* (2000), discusses the new genetics and its implications for ethics, especially as they concern issues of justice. Also noteworthy is Justine Burley and John Harris (eds.), *A Companion to Genethics* (2002). Ruth Chadwick, Mairi Levitt, and Darren Shickle (eds.), *The Right to Know and the Right Not to Know* (1997), a multidisciplinary research project in bioethics, examines issues relating to genetic information. Other issues are discussed in Norman Daniels, *Just Health Care* (1985); Len Doyal and Jeffrey S. Tobias (eds.), *Informed Consent in Medical Research* (2001); Jennifer Jackson, *Truth, Trust, and Medicine* (2001); and the journal *Developing World Bioethics*.

APPROACHES

Tom L. Beauchamp and James F. Childress, *Principles of Biomedical Ethics*, 5th ed. (2001), expounds and defends the "four principles" approach. Raanan Gillon (ed.), *Principles of Health Care Ethics* (1994), contains a large number of essays on the four principles and their application to different issues. Helga Kuhse, *Caring: Nurses, Women, and Ethics* (1997), is a critical account of the attempt to base nursing ethics on a feminine ethics of care. Edmund D. Pellegrino and David C. Thomasma, *The Virtues in Medical Practice* (1993), offers a virtue-based ethics for medicine and health care. Susan Sherwin, *No Longer Patient: Feminist Ethics and Health Care* (1992), is an exposition and defense of feminist bioethics.

POLICY MAKING

Examples of publications of policy-making bodies in bioethics include Human Genome Organisation, Ethical, Legal, and Social Issues Committee, *Statement on the Principled Conduct of Genetic Research* (1996), and *Statement on Stem Cells* (2004); United States National Bioethics Advisory Commission, *Ethical Issues in Human Stem Cell Research*, 3 vol. (1999–2000); and Nuffield Council on Bioethics, "Genetic Screening: Ethical Issues" (1993), and *The Ethics of Research Involving Animals* (2005).

GLOBAL BIOETHICS

Global bioethics is covered in *Bioethics: Special Issue: IV World Congress of the International Association of Bioethics* (July 1999).

BIBLIOGRAPHY

EUGENICS

Daniel J. Kevles, *In the Name of Eugenics: Genetics and the Uses of Human Heredity* (1985, reissued with a new preface, 1995), remains the cornerstone for all contemporary eugenics scholarship. Diane B. Paul, *Controlling Human Heredity: 1865 to the Present* (1995), serves as a superlative introduction. Mathew Thomson, *The Problem of Mental Deficiency: Eugenics, Democracy, and Social Policy in Britain, 1870–1959* (1998), analyzes many social dimensions of British eugenics. Robert Proctor, *Racial Hygiene: Medicine Under the Nazis* (1998), thoroughly explores the Nazi's eugenic-mindedness. Philip R. Sloan (ed.), *Controlling Our Destinies: Historical, Philosophical, Ethical, and Theological Perspectives on the Human Genome Project* (2000), provides a foundation work for discussion on the "new eugenics."

GENE THERAPY

A comprehensive introduction to gene therapy is Joseph Panno, *Gene Therapy: Treating Disease by Repairing Genes* (2005). Detailed coverage of the technologies employed in gene therapy is provided in Nancy Smyth Templeton (ed.), *Gene and Cell Therapy: Therapeutic Mechanisms and Strategies*, 3rd ed. (2009). Applications of gene therapy and mechanisms of gene delivery are discussed in David V. Schaffer and Weichang Zhou (eds.), *Gene Therapy and Gene Delivery Systems* (2005).

GENETIC COUNSELING

Information on genetic counseling is provided in Anthony R. Gregg and Joe Leigh Simpson (eds.), *Genetic Screening and Counseling* (2010). Texts dealing specifically with ethical issues in the field are Dianne M. Bartels, Bonnie S. LeRoy, and Arthur L. Caplan, *Genetic Counseling: Ethical Challenges and Consequences* (2011), originally published as *Prescribing Our Future* (1993); and Jonathan Glover, *Choosing Children: Genes, Disability, and Design* (2008). Background on the development of genetic counseling specifically in the United States is provided in Alexandra Minna Stern, *Telling Genes: The Story of Genetic Counseling in America* (2012).

HEREDITY

HISTORICAL TEXTS

Theodosius Dobzhansky, *Heredity and the Nature of Men* (1964), is an excellent discussion of classical genetics and its social and cultural implications. A.H. Sturtevant, *A History of Genetics* (1965, reissued 2001), is a review of the critical developments in the evolution of our understanding of heredity. James D. Watson, *The Double Helix: A Personal Account of the Discovery of the Structure of DNA* (1968, reissued 2001), available also in a critical edition edited by Gunther S. Stent (1980, reissued 1998), is written by one of DNA's discoverers.

MODERN HEREDITY AND GENETICS TEXTS

Paul Berg and Maxine Singer, *Dealing with Genes: The Language of Heredity* (1992), is a well-illustrated overview of molecular genetics and its relationship with developmental biology, medicine, and biochemistry. Michael R. Cummings, *Human Heredity: Principles and Issues*, 6th ed. (2002); and Anthony J.F. Griffiths et al., *Modern Genetic Analysis*, 2nd ed. (2002), are comprehensive textbooks.

HUMAN GENETIC DISEASE

James Wynbrandt and Mark D. Ludman, *The Encyclopedia of Genetic Disorders and Birth Defects*, 2nd ed. (2000); Benjamin A. Picrcc, *The Family Genetic Sourcebook* (1990); Karen Bellenir, *Genetic Disorders Sourcebook* (2000); and John F. Jackson, *Genetics and You* (1996), provide basic, easily understandable information on the principles of heredity and the causes, screening, and treatment of genetic disease. Raye Lynn Alford, *Genetics and Your Health: A Guide for the 21st Century* (1999), discusses recent advances in genetic research, including the Human Genome

Project, and its effects on the diagnosis and treatment of genetic disease. Doris Teichler-Zallen, *Does It Run in the Family? A Consumer's Guide to DNA Testing for Genetic Disorders* (1997), explains the biochemical bases of genetic tests and various policy issues surrounding their use. Harold Varmus and Robert A. Weinberg, *Genes and the Biology of Cancer* (1993), explores the genetic basis of the disease.

George H. Sack, Jr., *Medical Genetics* (1999); and Arthur P. Mange and Elaine Johansen Mange, *Genetics: Human Aspects*, 2nd ed. (1990), are informative, upper-level textbooks. Victor A. McKusick, *Mendelian Inheritance in Man: A Catalog of Human Genes and Genetic Disorders*, 12th ed. (1998), is a compendium of human genes and the mutations that cause disease.

NANOTECHNOLOGY

K. Eric Drexler, *Engines of Creation* (1987, reissued 1996), and *Nanosystems: Molecular Machinery, Manufacturing, and Computation* (1992), provide early and controversial views on how nanoscale mechanical systems might one day be used to build complex molecular structures. Scientific American, *Understanding Nanotechnology* (2003), is a highly accessible perspective on major areas of science and technology likely to be affected by nanotechnology. The following books are good basic introductions to nanomaterials, nanoproperties, and potential applications: Michael

BIBLIOGRAPHY

Wilson et al., *Nanotechnology: Basic Science and Emerging Technologies* (2002); and Charles P. Poole, Jr., and Frank J. Owens, *Introduction to Nanotechnology* (2003). William A. Goddard III (ed.), *Handbook of Nanoscience, Engineering, and Technology* (2003), gives an in-depth view of selected areas of nanotechnology, including molecular electronics, assembly, and mechanics.

The following books emphasize biological perspectives and applications for nanotechnology: Michael Gross, *Travels to the Nanoworld: Miniature Machinery in Nature and Technology* (1999, reissued 2001); Edward A. Rietman, *Molecular Engineering of Nanosystems* (2001); and Robert A. Freitas, Jr., *Basic Capabilities* (1999), vol. 1, and *Biocompatibility* (2003), vol. 2, of *Nanomedicine*.

INDEX

A

achondroplasia, 36, 37, 38
additions
    chromosomal, 9, 10, 28, 30
alcohol
    and genetic damage, 56, 61–62
allelic heterogeneity, 38
allelic homogeneity, 38
alphafetoprotein
    and genetic testing, 82–83
amniocentesis, 74, 82, 83–84, 88
amyotrophic lateral sclerosis, 66
Angelman syndrome, 44, 47
anticipation
    in non-Mendelian inheritance, 45–46

B

back mutation, 19
bacteria
    and genetic damage, 56, 57–58
balanced translocation carrier, 72
Barr body, 31
bioassays, 103–106
biochemical tests
    and prenatal testing, 92
bioethics
    approaches in, 153–155
    contemporary and traditional ethical theories, 149–153
    general issues in, 134–138
    global approaches, 157–158
    particular issues in health care, 138–139
    and policy making, 156–157
    and public attitudes, 155–156
    social and legal issues, 143–149
    traditional philosophical questions, 139–143
    what it is, 129–133
breast cancer
    familial, 51–52
Burkitt lymphoma, 53–54

C

cancer
    genetics of, 49–54
cell division
    chromosomal behavior during, 3–6
chorionic villus sampling, 74, 83, 84, 87, 88
chromosomal aberrations
    numerical, 25, 26–27, 28
    of sex chromosomes, 25, 29–34
    structural, 8–10, 25, 27–28
chromosomes
    behavior during cell division, 3–6
    what they are, 2
chronic granulomatous disease, 65–66

INDEX

chronic myelogenous leukemia, 53
cloning, 89–90, 99, 107–115, 121, 123, 129, 141–142
codons, 17
cognitive and behavioral genetics, 54–55
colorectal cancer
  familial, 51, 52, 78
combustion products
  and genetic damage, 22, 56, 59–60
comparative genomic hybridization (CGH), 86, 89
cri-du-chat syndrome, 9–10
Crick, Francis, 12, 14
cystic fibrosis, 79, 92, 94, 119

D

deletions
  chromosomal, 9–10, 28, 29
depurination, 22
DNA
  cloning, 107–115
  and gene mutation, 19–22
  and the genetic code, 16–19
  and heredity, 11
  structure and composition, 11–12, 16
DNA fingerpring, 117
DNA tests
  prenatal, 89, 92
Down syndrome, 26, 27, 28, 72, 74, 82, 89
duplications
  chromosomal, 10

E

enol, 21
environmental agents
  types of genetic damage caused by them, 55–66
ethics of care, 151, 152–153
eugenics, 68, 75, 81, 131, 134–138

F

fluorescence in situ hybridization (FISH), 85–86, 89, 95
48,XXXY syndrome, 34
49,XXXXY syndrome, 34
47,XYY syndrome, 34
forward mutation, 19
four-principles approach in bioethics, 153–155
fragile-X syndrome, 44, 46
Franklin, Rosalind, 14–15
fungi
  and genetic damage, 56, 57–58

G

genealogy
  and genetic testing, 91
gene doping, 120
gene therapy
  and cloning, 99, 107–114, 121, 123, 129, 141–142
  future of, 119–121
  genomics, 117–118
  and human genome

mapping, 97–99
and induced pluripotent stem cells, 97, 99, 121, 124–127
and nanotechnology, 101–106
prerequisites for, 99, 101
and recombinant DNA, 106–107, 108–113, 115–117, 119
regulation of clinical trials, 99, 100
and somatic cell nuclear transfer, 121–124
genetic heterogeneity, 38
genetic counseling
in adulthood, 78–80
in infancy, 75–78
prenatal, 71–75
what it is, 67–70, 144–146
genetic testing
after the neonatal period, 92–95
prenatal, 81–92, 116
types of, 80–81
genomics, 117–118
genotype
what it is, 1–2

H

hemophilia, 42–43, 92, 134
Hippocratic Oath, 131, 133
human genome
mapping, 91, 97–99, 117
Human Genome Project, 91, 97, 137
Huntington disease, 44, 46, 80, 92

I

inborn errors of metabolism, 39–41, 77
induced pluripotent stem cells
and gene therapy, 124–127
industrial chemicals
and genetic damage, 56, 58–59
ionizing radiation
and genetic damage, 22, 56, 63–64, 76
isomer, 20

K

Kantian ethics, 131, 151–152, 154
karyotyping, 28, 29, 34, 72, 73, 83, 85, 87–89, 95
keto, 20, 21
Klinefelter syndrome, 30, 31–33, 34, 89

L

"labs-on-chips," 105–106
leaky mutations, 20
Lyon, Mary, 31

M

maternal serum tests, 82
meiosis, 2, 4–6, 7, 9, 10, 27, 119
meiotic disjunction, 26
Mendel, Gregor, 35

172

INDEX

microarray hybridization analysis, 95
Miescher, Johann Friedrich, 11
mitochondrial DNA, 17, 91
mitosis, 2, 3–4
molecular genetics, 10–22
molecular oxygen
  and genetic damage, 64–66
mosaicism, 27, 29, 31, 33
multifactorial inheritance
  diseases caused by, 24, 48–49, 50, 72, 73
mutagens, 22, 58, 62, 64, 65
mutations
  in DNA, 19–22

N

nanoparticles
  magnetic, 104–105
nanoscale pores, 106
nanoshells, 103
nanotechnology, 101–106
nonpenetrant carriers, 39
null mutations, 20

O

oncogenes, 50, 53, 56, 76
organic dendrimers, 102–103

P

pedigree, 35, 36, 41, 42, 68, 69, 70, 72
percutaneous umbilical blood sampling, 86
phenotype
  what it is, 1–2
phenylketonuria, 39–41, 77, 92
Philadelphia chromosome, 53
plants
  and genetic damage, 56, 57–58
polymerase chain reaction (PCR), 85, 89, 95
Prader-Willi syndrome, 44, 47, 89
preimplantation genetic diagnosis, 83, 85, 86
protein manufacture
  and gene therapy, 119

R

recombinant DNA technology
  and cloning, 107–113
  and diagnostics, 115–117
  and DNA tests, 89–90
  and genomics, 117
  and protein manufacture, 119
  and reverse genetics, 115
  what it is, 106–107
restriction fragment length polymorphisms, 117
retinoblastoma, 50–51

S

saviour siblings, 150–151
sickle cell anemia, 39, 79, 92, 94
single-gene Mendelian

inheritance and diseases
autosomal dominant
  inherited diseases, 35–39
autosomal recessive
  inherited diseases, 39–41
sex-linked inherited
  diseases, 7–8, 41–43
single-gene non-Mendelian
inheritance and diseases
  imprinted gene mutations,
    44, 47–48
  mitochondrial DNA
    mutations, 44, 46–47
  triplet repeat expansion
    disorders, 44–46
single nucleotide
  polymorphisms tests, 91
somatic cell nuclear transfer,
  121–124
Southern blotting, 95
synaptonemal complex, 9

T

Tay-Sachs disease, 79, 86,
  136, 142
thalassemia, 79
traits
  linkage of, 6–8
trisomy x, 34
tumour suppressor genes 50,
  51, 52, 76
Turner syndrome, 29, 89

twins
  and nature versus nurture,
    54–55

U

ultrasound
  as noninvasive genetic
    testing, 82
ultraviolet radiation
  and genetic damage, 22, 56,
    62–63
uniparental disomy, 48
utilitarianism, 151, 154

V

variable number tandem
  repeats, 117
virtue ethics, 151, 152
viruses
  and genetic damage, 22,
    56–57

W

Watson, James, 12, 14
Wilkins, Maurice, 14, 15

X

X inactivation, 30–31, 34, 43

Y

Y chromosome testing, 91